FOUNDER AND PRESIDENT
Patricia Tarr

EDITOR AND ART DIRECTOR
J. Abbott Miller
Design/Writing/Research, New York

EDITORIAL ASSISTANTS
Tracey Hummer
Emily Miller

DIRECTOR OF ONLINE SERVICES
Jeff Tarr Jr.

Financial support is derived from individual and foundation contributions and reader subscriptions. Dance Ink, Inc., is a tax-exempt organization under section 501(c)(3) of the Internal Revenue Code. Contributions to Dance Ink, Inc., are tax deductible to the extent provided by law.

SUBSCRIPTION INFORMATION
One Year $36 \ Two Years $72

2wice
214 Sullivan Street 6c
New York, NY 10012
t : 212 228 0540
f : 212 228 0654

© 1997 **2wice** All Rights Reserved

[1047–823X]

PRINTED IN THE UNITED STATES BY
The Studley Press, Inc.
P.O. Box 214 151 East Housatonic Street
Dalton, MA 01226 \ 413 684 0441

CURRENT COPIES ARE DISTRIBUTED
TO BOOKSTORES
D.A.P. Magazines (Distributed Art Publishers)
155 Avenue of the Americas, 2nd floor
New York, NY 10013

COVERS
{front} James Wojcik, *Toe Jam*, 1997. model: Michael Alan Ross

{back} Jan Van Eyck, *The Arnolfini Wedding* (detail), 1434. Oil on panel, 32 1/4 x 23 1/2 inches, National Gallery, London. Courtesy of Bridgeman/Art Resource, NY.

{inside covers} Theo Coulombe, from Painted Feet, The Mendhi Project, 1996. Courtesy of Bridges and Bodell Gallery.

2wice

VISUAL \ CULTURE \ DOCUMENT
VOL : 1 \ NO : 1

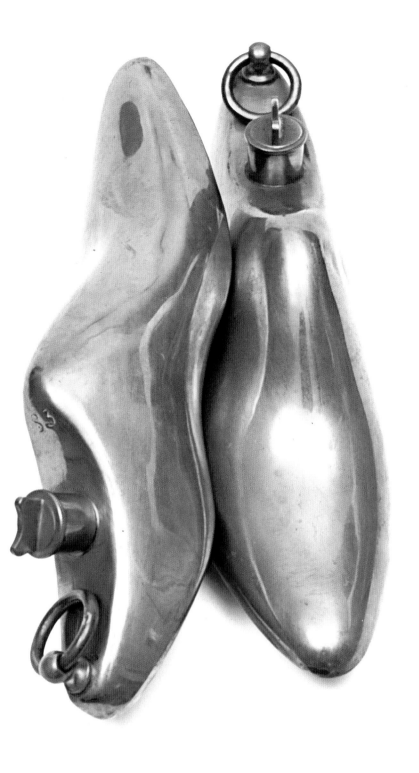

Contents

ACKNOWLEDGMENTS
Joanna Astor, Javan Bayer, Susan Bennis, Dr. John Bergmann, Margaret Bodell, Gaza Bowen, Dr. Stanley Burns, Adam Boxer, Dominic Calabrese, Andrea Codrington, Brenda Cullerton, Leon Dalva, Nancy Dalva, Dr. Eric Delson, Angela Edgar, Warren Edwards, Tracy Eller, Margit Erb, Joyce Faust, Kasper Fleischmann, Sidney Fortner, Robert Full, Alison Gallup, Laura Gens, Dorothy Globus, RoseLee Goldberg, Laura Giammarco, Robert Gurbo, Erica Granchalek, Laura Jacobs, Spina Heilman, Annie Heminway, Dr. Howard Hillstrom, Lisa Hintzpeter, Laura Jacobs, Recinda Jeannine, Anne Kain, John-Paul Kernot, Jan Kesner, Constantine Kesting, Danielle Korwin, Rosalind Krauss, Hermann Lademann, Maud Lavin, Howard Levy, Natasha Lunn, Ellen Lupton, Lee Marks, Richard Martin, Diana McCain, Patricia Mears, Misty Moye, Geoff Nicholson, Malika Noui, Linda O'Keeffe, Michael Pollak, Cheryl Pflanzer, Marc Raibert, Nancy Rexford, Paula Richter, Glenn Roberts, Thea Cadabra-Rooke, Loretta Roome, Michael Alan Ross, Richard Ross, Dr. Frank Rossi, Alyssa Sachar, Gillian Scalander, Robert Serling, Ellen Sirot, Stephanie Spalding, Sheila Stone, Valerie Steele, June Swann, Dr. Frederick Szalay, Barbara Tannenbaum, Alice Tassel, Ken Turino, James Traeger, Louise Coffey-Webb, Barbara Williams, Jonathan Wolford, Ivan Vartanian

Italian neoclassical gilded armchair
with winged lion armrest support
and lion paw foot, circa 1810.
Collection of Dalva Brothers Inc.,
New York.

PHOTOGRAPHS BY
JOSEF ASTOR

natural history

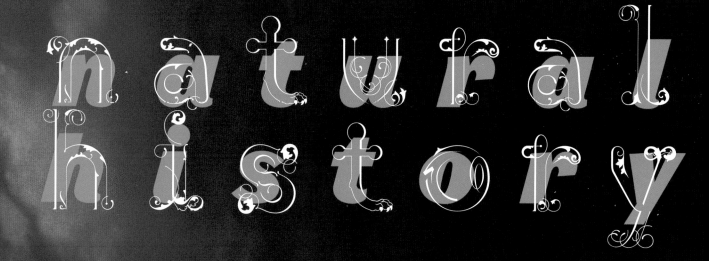

Left to right: Spanish rococo blue
laquered sidechair with ball and claw
foot, circa 1750; lion paw from a French
Directoire painted bed, circa 1790;
Charles X sidechair with deer hoof leg,
circa 1830. Collection of Dalva Brothers,
Inc., New York.

Richard Ross, *Stunt Dummies*, Ellis Merchantile prop storage warehouse, Hollywood, CA, 1989.

Frida Kahlo, *What the Water Gave Me,* **1938.** Oil on canvas, 38 x 30 inches. Dolores Olmedo Collection, Mexico City. Courtesy of Schalkwijk/Art Resource, NY

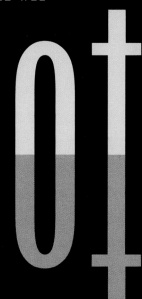

HERE IS THE CHURCH/HERE IS THE STEEPLE/
OPEN THE DOORS/AND SEE ALL THE PEOPLE.

HUMANS LEARN EARLY THAT THEIR HANDS ARE GODLY, THEIR FINGERS DIVINE. There are hands that make candles and hands that light them, hands that build churches and cities and space ships and steeples, hands that fold in prayer.

THIS LITTLE PIGGY WENT TO MARKET/THIS LITTLE PIGGY STAYED HOME/
THIS LITTLE PIGGY HAD ROAST BEEF/THIS LITTLE PIGGY HAD NONE/
AND THIS LITTLE PIGGY WENT 'WEE-WEE-WEE-WEE'
ALL THE WAY HOME.

SO MUCH FOR THE FOOT. We learn early that feet are not in the same league with hands. Baby feet are pudgy, chubby, fleshy, piggy, with snub toes like peas from a pod. Baby feet are inarticulate (wee-wee!) and eminently edible (beefy!)—what mother hasn't nibbled her putto's foot? But hands, no matter how little, are not for mommy's nibbling.

POOR FEET, SO LOW ON THE TOTEM POLE.
In our admiration for the human hand, a structure highly social and always within view (even exhibitionist), its motor refinement a flamboyant standard against which all other motor refinements can be measured, we forget that the foot is every bit as definitive as the hand in our leap to human status. Maybe even more so. Giving both Satan and the reader a first glimpse of Adam and Eve in the garden in *Paradise Lost* (Book IV, line 285), notice what John Milton chooses to accentuate:

"...THE FIEND
SAW UNDELIGHTED ALL DELIGHT, ALL KIND
OF LIVING CREATURES, NEW TO SIGHT AND STRANGE.
TWO OF FAR NOBLER SHAPE, ERECT AND TALL,
GOD-LIKE ERECT, WITH NATIVE HONOUR CLAD
IN NAKED MAJESTY, SEEMED LORDS OF ALL"

GOD-LIKE ERECT! It's a Miltonian thunderbolt of awe—almost an expletive. And Milton is as true to evolutionary science as he is to Genesis. Man is the only creature on earth that is fully bipedal. While there are other opposable thumbs to be found in nature, we alone have a foot that permits continuous upright walking.

WHAT MAKES A FOOT HUMAN? It is a question anthropologists still grapple with. In a master's thesis published as recently as 1996, Avelin A. Malyango reexamined the 1.8 million-year-old *Homo habilis* OH 8 foot from Olduvai Gorge, Tanzania, and ended a long-standing controversy by proving that this foot was without question a habitual bipedal foot.[1] His analysis showed that the range of its ankle articulations was fixed more narrowly than in a foot adapted for tree climbing; that the big toe was aligned with the other toes, and that the baby-toe side of the foot has become remarkably robust—a stabilizing balance to the big-toe side. An arch was detectable.

In short, he argued, this foot offered equilibrium and leverage on the rough surface of the ground.

As for why the foot evolved, Malyango explains that "we are very closely related to African apes. Through the evolutionary process the human being moved from the forest—coming to the ground to look for food. If you are on the ground walking with four feet, you can't see the predators around you. But if you are walking upright, you can see all the area. If you spend more time walking upright from four legs, you have to modify yourself. And not only in terms of upright walking: Human beings by this time were increasing their brain volume. So there was modification in the foot, the limb, the brain.

"Now why should they depend more on the legs to stand up and to walk, as compared to the chimpanzee? Because by this time the human being was carrying tools. All these processes were important in the transition from the quadrupedal foot to the human foot."

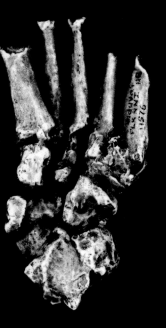

OH 8 (Homo habilis) fossil foot. Courtesy of and © Frederick Szalay and Eric Delson, City University of New York.

In fact, one theory posits that the evolution of the human brain is highly associated with meat eating, and that it was meat that man was hunting—with tools—in the grasses. This theory is not airtight (why then didn't the brains of big cats evolve?), but Malyango speaks for most paleoanthropologists when he says, "We believe that difficulty in acquiring food was the most important trigger mechanism for evolution." In other words, this little piggy went to market.

Turning to the pages of that classic text, *Gray's Anatomy,* we find Milton meeting up with Malyango: "The foot is constructed on the same principles as the hand," writes Dr. Henry Gray, "but modified to form a firm basis of support for the rest of the body when in the erect position." Gray points out that the foot is placed at right angles to the leg—"a position which is almost peculiar to man"—and then goes on to sing the praises of that feature which is entirely peculiar to man: the arch. Technically called the LONGITUDINAL ARCH, we all know it as the curved indentation that rises along the inside length of each foot. The human arch is a high-tension bridge that arcs from heel (the true Atlas) to ball (the Baryshnikov of foot parts). And it is, as well, that absence of flesh which gives our footprint the look of a figure eight drawn by Miró. Is the arch a solid or a space? Plato's Cave or Chartres Cathedral?

Reading Gray, you feel it is the latter. For when he writes about the TRANSVERSE ARCH—the second arch (located at the hinder part of the metatarsus) without which a foot is not human—he says it "can scarcely be described as a true arch, but presents more the character of a half-dome." Right angles! Domes! Arcs! Architecture! One can't help thinking of the

1. The female hominid famously known as Lucy (species Australopithecus afarensis, 3.9 million years old) is older than Homo habilis and is thought to have been both terrestrial and arboreal. Lucy's hands are cupped like an apes and the phalanges are long, for climbing. But Lucy's pelvis is flared like a human pelvis and her vertebrae curved, a feature of bipedalism. Except for a piece of talus, Lucy's feet are missing.

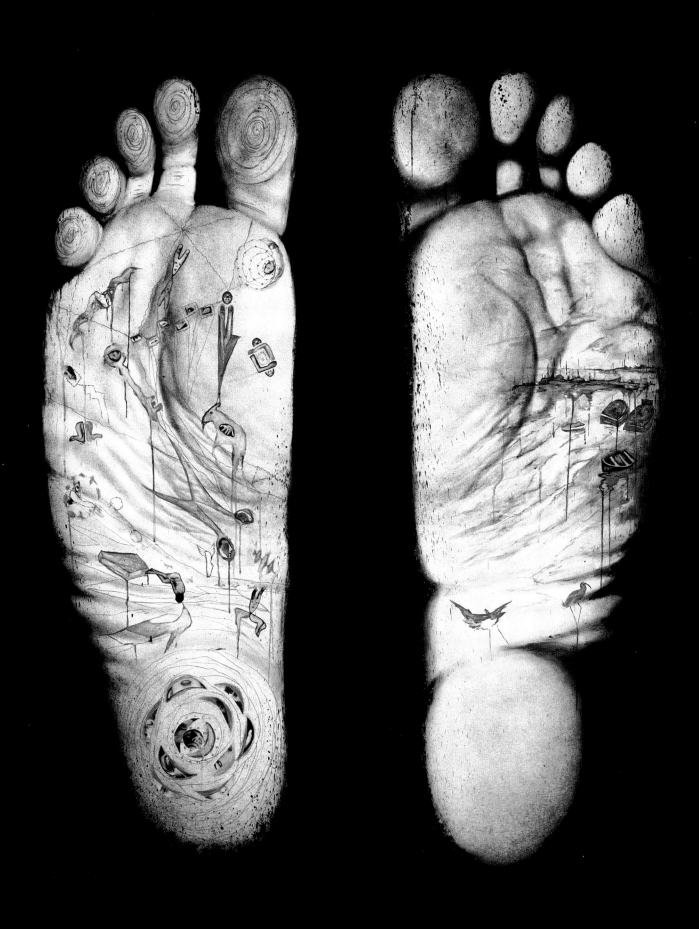

Annette Messager, *Mes Trophées* **(My Trophies), 1987.** Acrylic and pastel on black and white photographs. Courtesy of the Los Angeles County Museum of Art. Purchased with funds provided by the Ralph M. Parsons Fund, Clyde and Karen Beswick, Linda and Jerry Janger, Ronnie and Vidal Sassoon, Sharleen Cooper Cohen, David and Susan Gersh, and Bonnie Wilke.

Egyptians with their subterranean arches and vaults (used in tombs but never temples), the Etruscans and their inspired city gate, Porta Augusta, the first example of an arch integrated, dignified, within a larger structure, and the Romans, who, in their mastery of the arch, were able to create immense interior spaces.

And interior space is the deep beauty of the human foot. For the arch not only allowed us to rise up and behold what would normally have been beyond view, it was integral to inward seeing—liberating the hands, the mind, the imagination. The arch in our foot mimes the curved surface of the earth. It takes us where we want to go, yet never empties its inside pocket of solitude, secrecy—the quest in every step. I have often felt that the sylphs and fairies and wilis of ballet actually sleep in that little grotto under the ballerina's arch, released into the air when she goes up on pointe. Look to ancient art and you see the arch beginning to appear in Egyptian bas reliefs, a mystic sliver of shadow caught under a working wedge of foot. Skip to classical Greek sculpture—the Charioteer from the Sanctuary of Apollo at Delphi, for instance—and you see enlightenment, arches sprung high as a hemisphere.

We rarely think of the foot in such ethereal terms. We pay little heed to the grandeur of our arch, which, reinvented by builders, is the simplest, greatest weight-bearing structure of civilization. Even those who work in classical dance today seem not to understand the infinity factor implicit in the arch. Piggies, dogs, mules—such slang terms catch the common perception of feet as beasts of burden. For while the hands flit around town, Isadora-like, innocently naked and expressively free, the feet of most people are uniformed in shoes, coupled like galley slaves (toes faced forward, always, nose to the grindstone).

Sotades, *The Charioteer*, 5th century BC. Bronze. Archeological Museum, Delphi, Greece. Courtesy Nimatallah/ Art Resource, NY.

Fragment of a bas-relief depicting a dancer. Vatican Museums, Vatican State. Courtesy of Alinari/Art Resource, NY.

ITS SPECTACULAR ANATOMY ASIDE, the foot is in constant discourse with dirt, gravel, cement, rainwater, mud, earth. Bare, it gets as soiled as a vegetable, as dusty as a hoof. Shod, it stews in scents of moisture mixed with wool, leather, and nylon (meanwhile the pampered hand dabs perfume at its wrist). Mothers tell of the stab of sadness felt when putting baby into those first stiff leather shoes—like putting a puppy into a harness. Look at the names we give afflictions of the foot: corns, bunions, hammer toes, clubfoot, pigeon toes, duck feet. When the images aren't plant or animal, they are hammers and clubs, the blunt instruments of manual labor, the first tools of early man.

Cave or cathedral, bestial or godlike? Ambivalence is built into our feelings about the foot, which is why the washing of another's feet is an act both humble and hallowed. In the example Jesus gives to his disciples in John 13, washing their feet during the Last Supper, we see Simon Peter refusing the service, and then bargaining: "not my feet only; wash my hands and head as well." To which Jesus replies, "A man who has bathed needs no further washing." The washed foot is commensurate with moral cleanliness.

No doubt it is this embodiment of oppositions that makes the foot ripe for metaphor. In the form of shoes, of course, feet wear many guises: skates, stilts, stilettos, pointes, boots, cleats, taps, wing tips, brogues, slippers, flippers—the list is endless. But even a bare foot enjoys poetic consideration, simply because it is more creaturely than the hand, more often covered up and mysterious. If the waist is the equator, feet are in the exotic, hot, and unmapped southern hemisphere, head and heart and hands up north.

AMBIVALENCE IS BUILT INTO OUR FEELINGS ABOUT THE FOOT, WHICH IS WHY THE WASHING OF ANOTHER'S FEET IS AN ACT BOTH HUMBLE AND HALLOWED.

BECAUSE FEET ARE SOUTH OF THE BORDER, in the grasses, they are the site of sexual associations. Though the foot is without gender, structurally the same in both men and women, it is also phallic in shape, with the shoe acting as womb or room (hence the odd, equalizing twist in the Cinderella story, where she is in possession of the phallus, and he, the Prince, has the slipper in his pocket). The practice of Chinese foot binding, banned for pain and purposelessness, has parallels in modern day genital mutilation. It's a connection the Chinese had made long ago—they thought foot binding tightened the vagina. Going beyond metaphor, foot binding turned the female foot into a second genital, made the arch into a hole. The process required the breaking and continuous crimping of the metatarsals. The history of foot binding might be called *The Rape of the Arch*. As for its frequent equation with the toe shoe of classical dance, that analogy is superficial and flawed. Pointe work celebrates the Olympian physiology of a healthy human arch.

"See that every wall . . . has its foundations on the ground or on well-planted arches," writes Leonardo da Vinci in his *Notebooks*, describing the proper way to design the palace of a prince. Moving from architecture to anatomy, he keeps returning to the foot as a measure or a mean, and reports that: "The whole foot will go between the elbow and the wrist, and between the elbow and the inner angle of the arm . . . The foot is as long as the whole head of the man, that is, from beneath the chin to the very top of the head." Obsessively, Leonardo calibrates the proportions of feet (with and without toes) compared to hands (with and without fingers) and gets to a giddy, amazing, maniacal minutiae: "The length of the longest toe from where it begins to be divided from the big toe to its extremity . . . is equal to the width of the mouth." Who knew?!

PROPORTIONS ARE NOT LEONARDO-PERFECT in the Renaissance masterpiece *The Expulsion from Paradise*, a fresco in the Brancacci Chapel in Florence. But then its painter, Masaccio, was busy solving other problems. In *The Lives of the Artists*, Giorgio Vasari praises Masaccio's innovations in perspective painting, especially where the feet were concerned: ". . . he felt that all figures which do not stand with their feet flat and foreshortened, but are on the tips of their toes, are destitute of all excellence and style in essentials, and show an utter ignorance of foreshortening."

In Masaccio's rendering of unrecoverable loss, the feet are indeed foreshortened, Eve's so much as to appear crude, not quite differentiated from the barren earth she trods. Adam, however, steps out with a foot in bold profile, the left. And look where his right foot is: poised on the threshold of that high, slim, almost surreal, keyhole of a door, the portal to Paradise—an arch. Masaccio has caught man in anguish between two states; Adam's right foot is the hinge between grace and disgrace, between mindless life and mortal weight. But is all really lost? Above the couple, the archangel Michael spreads his arms in a canopy of comfort, a makeshift arch. And below, though Adam and Eve's hands are grave and guilty, busy with the business of shame, their feet carry them forward, striding straight into the sun. "Some natural tears they dropped, but wiped them soon," writes Milton in his poem's last lines. "The world was all before them."

LAURA JACOBS *is a contributing editor at* Vanity Fair, *and writes on the performing arts and fashion for* The New Criterion, The New Republic, *and* Stagebill.

Masaccio, *The Expulsion from Paradise*, ca. 1425. Fresco. The Brancacci Chapel, Santa Maria del Carmine, Florence. Courtesy of Erich Lessing/Art Resource, NY.

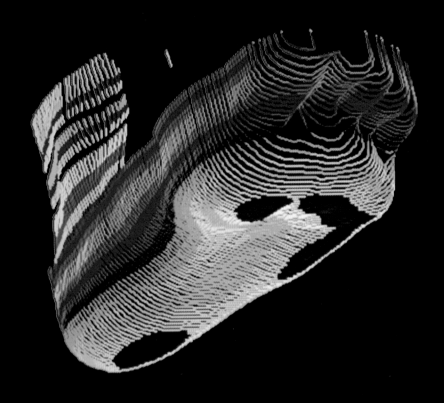

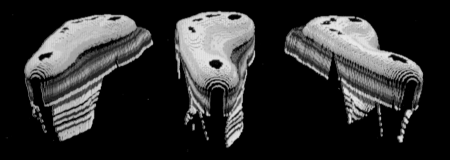

Images made by the Bergmann Optical Laser Foot Scanner, Model 2001.
Courtesy of Dr. John Bergmann, Bergmann Orthotic Laboratory, Inc., Glenview, IL.

Arno Rafael Minkkinen, *self-portrait, Fosters Pond,* 1990. © Arno Rafael Minkkinen. Courtesy Houk Friedman Gallery, New York.

Arno Rafael Minkkinen, *Self-portrait, Fosters Pond,* 1989. © Arno Rafael Minkkinen. Courtesy of Houk Friedman Gallery, New York.

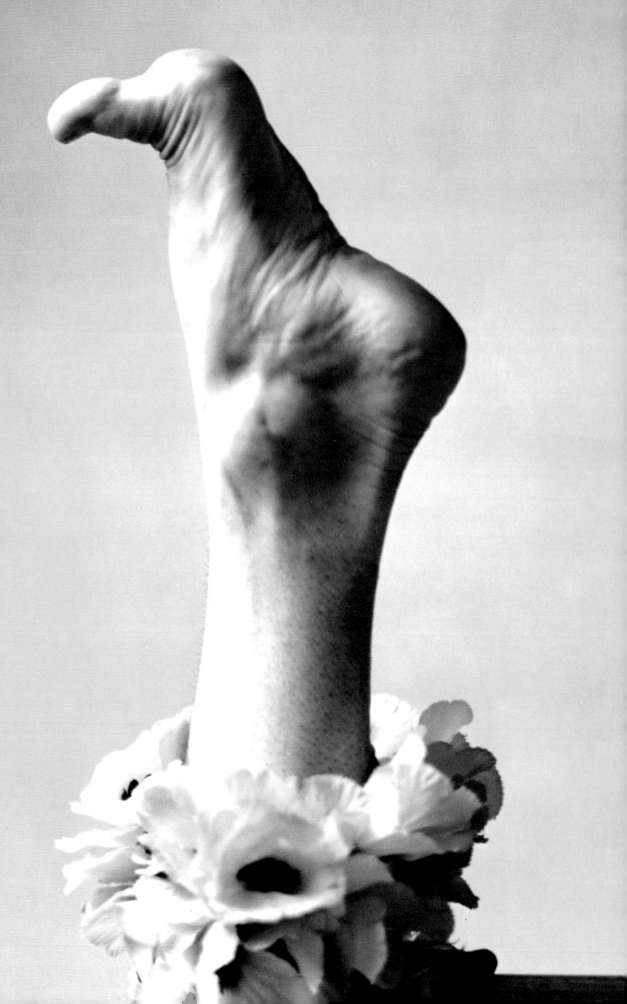

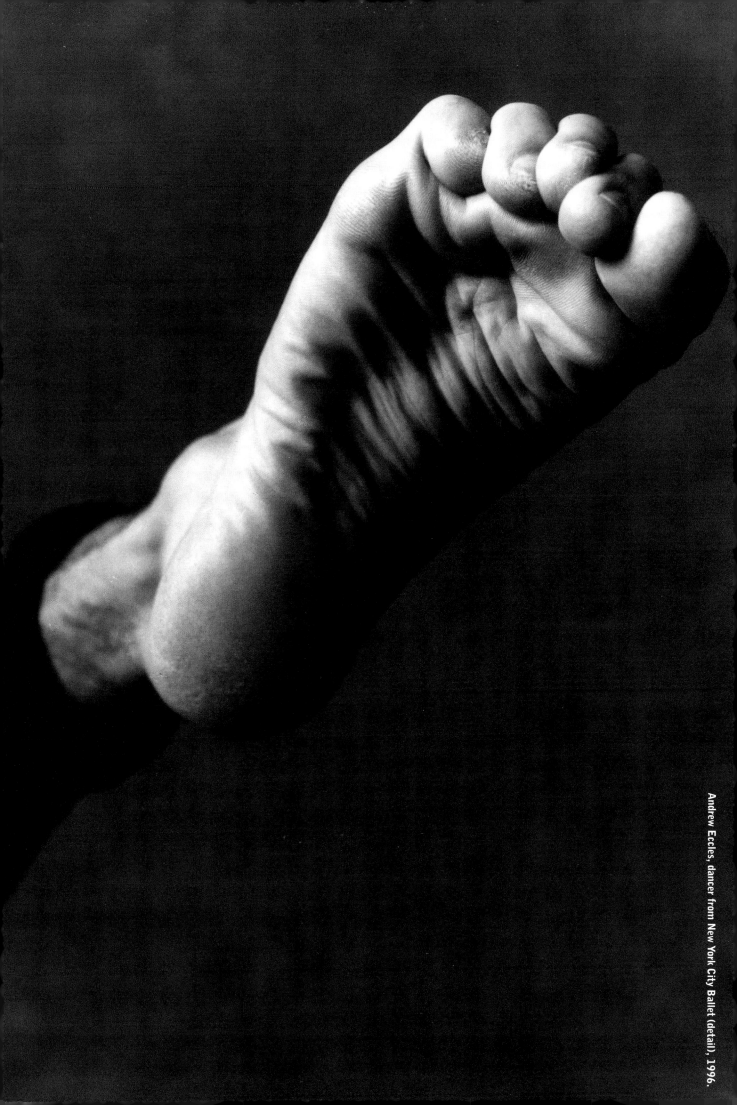

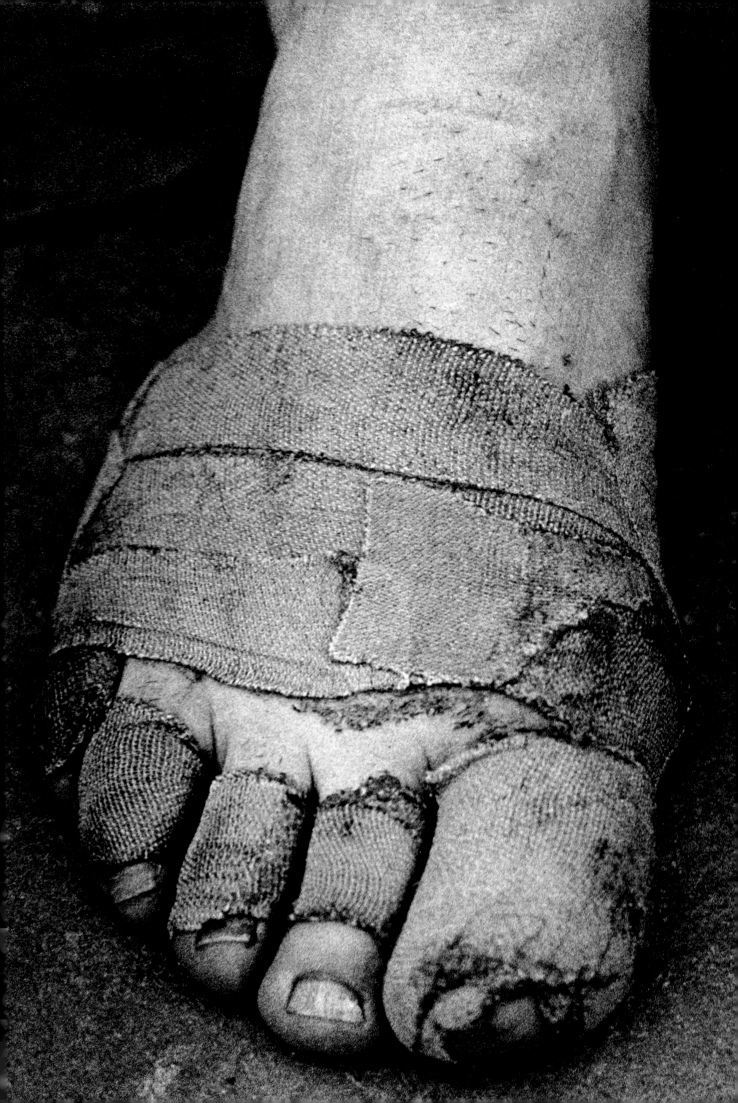

the human body... imagine a tide that will permanently elevate them, ...ever to return, into pure space. Human life entails, ... fact, the rage of seeing oneself as a back-and-... forth movement from refuse to the ideal, and from ... the ideal to refuse—a rage that is easily directed ... against an organ as base as the foot. ...The human foot is commonly subjected to ... grotesque tortures that deform it and make it rick-... In an imbecilic way it is doomed to corns, cal-... es, and bunions, and if one takes into account ... of phrase that are only now disappearing, ... the most nauseating filthiness; the peasant ... expression "her hands are as dirty as feet," while ... no longer true of the entire human collectivity, ... in the seventeenth century.

... whatever the role played in the erection of his ... nations for the tendency to conceal its length ... form as much as possible. Heels of greater or ... lesser height, depending on the sex, distract from ... the foot's low and flat character.

Besides, this uneasiness is often confused with a ... uneasiness; this is especially striking among ... Chinese, who, after having atrophied the feet ... women, situate them at the most excessive point ... The husband himself must not see the ... of his wife, and it is incorrect and ... in general to look at the feet of women. ... confessors, adapting themselves to this ... ask their Chinese penitents "if they ... looked at women's feet."

... aberration is found among the Turks ... Turks of Central Asia), who consider it ... show their nude feet and who even go ... to ... stockings.

... similar can be cited from classical ... apart from the use of very high soles in ... The most prudish Roman matrons con-... their toes to be seen. On the other ... concerning the feet developed exces-... modern era and only started to disap-... seventeenth century, M. Salomon Reinach ... its development in detail in the article ... pudiques" ["Modest Feet"], insisting ... of Spain, where women's feet have ... object of the most dreaded anxiety and ... the cause of crimes.¹ The simple fact of

THE BIG TOE

GEORGES BATAILLE

{1933}

THE BIG TOE is the most *human* part of the human body, in the sense that no other element of this body is as differentiated from the corresponding element of the anthropoid ape (chimpanzee, gorilla, orangutan, or gibbon). This is due to the fact that the ape is tree dwelling, whereas man moves on the earth without clinging to branches, having himself become a tree, in other words raising himself straight up in the air like a tree, and all the more beautiful for the correctness of his erection. In addition, the function of the human foot consists in giving a firm foundation to the erection of which man is so proud (the big toe, ceasing to grasp branches, is applied to the ground on the same plane as the other toes).

But whatever the role played in the erection by his foot, man, who has a light head, in other words a head raised to the heavens and heavenly things, sees it as split, on the pretext that he has his foot in the mud.

———

ALTHOUGH WITHIN THE BODY blood flows in equal quantities from high to low and from low to high, there is a bias in favor of that which elevates itself, and human life is erroneously seen as an elevation. The division of the universe into subterranean hell and perfectly pure heaven is an indelible conception, mud and darkness being the *principles* of evil as light and celestial space are the *principles* of good: with their feet in mud and their heads more or less in light, men obstinately imagine a tide that will permanently elevate them, never to return, into pure space. Human life entails, in fact, the rage of seeing oneself as a back-and-forth movement from refuse to the ideal, and from the ideal to refuse—a rage that is easily directed against an organ as *base* as the foot.

The human foot is commonly subjected to grotesque tortures that deform it and make it rickety. In an imbecilic way it is doomed to corns, calluses, and bunions, and if one takes into account turns of phrase that are only now disappearing, to the most nauseating filthiness: the peasant expression "her hands are as dirty as feet," while no longer true of the entire human collectivity, was so in the seventeenth century.

Man's secret horror of his foot is one of the explanations for the tendency to conceal its length and form as much as possible. Heels of greater or lesser height, depending on the sex, distract from the foot's low and flat character.

Besides, this uneasiness is often confused with a sexual uneasiness; this is especially striking among the Chinese, who, after having atrophied the feet of women, situate them at the most excessive point of deviance. The husband himself must not see the nude feet of his wife, and it is incorrect and immoral in general to look at the feet of women. Catholic confessors, adapting themselves to this aberration, ask their Chinese penitents "if they have not looked at women's feet."

The same aberration is found among the Turks (Volga Turks, Turks of Central Asia), who consider it immoral to show their nude feet and who even go to bed in stockings.

Nothing similar can be cited from classical antiquity (apart from the use of very high soles in tragedies). The most prudish Roman matrons constantly allowed their toes to be seen. On the other hand, modesty concerning the feet developed excessively in the modern era and only started to disappear in the nineteenth century. M. Salomon Reinach has studied this development in detail in the article entitled "Pieds pudiques" ["Modest Feet"], insisting on the role of Spain, where women's feet have been the object of the most dreaded anxiety and thus were the cause of crimes.[1] The simple fact of

1. In *L'Anthropologie*, 1903, pp.733-36; reprinted in *Cultes, mythes et religions*, 1905, vol 1, pp.105-10.

sion and gives a very shrill expression to the disorder of the human body, that product of the violent discord of the organs.

THE FORM OF THE BIG TOE is not, however, specifically monstrous, in this it is different than other parts of the body, the inside of a gaping mouth, for example. Only secondary (but common) deformations have been able to give its ignominy an exceptionally burlesque value. Now it is easy, most often, to account for burlesque values by means of extreme seductiveness. But we are led here to distinguish categorically two radically opposed kinds of seductiveness (whose habitual confusion entails the most absurd misunderstandings of language).

If a seductive element is to be attributed to the big toe, it is evidently not one to satisfy such exalted aspirations as, for example, the perfectly indelible taste that, in most cases, leads one to prefer elegant and correct forms. On the contrary, if one chooses, for example, the case of the Count of Villamediana, one can confirm that the pleasure he derived from touching the queen's foot specifically derived from the ugliness and infection represented by the baseness of the foot, in practice by most deformed feet. Thus, supposing that the queen's foot was perfectly pretty, it still derived its sacrilegious charm from deformed and muddy feet. Since a queen is a priori a more ideal and ethereal being than any other, it was human to the point of laceration to touch what in fact was not very different from the stinking foot of a thug. Here one submits to a seduction radically opposed to that caused by light and ideal beauty; the two orders of seduction are often confused because a person constantly moves from one to the other, and, given this back and forth movement, whether it finds its ends in one direction or the other, seduction is all the more acute when the movement is more brutal.

As for the big toe, classic foot fetishism leading to the licking of toes categorically indicates that it is a phenomenon of base seduction, which accounts for the burlesque value that is always more or less attached to the pleasures condemned by pure and superficial men.

THE MEANING OF THIS ARTICLE lies in its insistence on a direct and explicit questioning of seductiveness, without taking into account poetic concoctions that are, ultimately, nothing but a diversion (most human beings are naturally feeble and can only abandon themselves to their instincts when in a poetic haze). A return to reality does not imply any new acceptances, but means that one is seduced in a base manner, without transpositions and to the point of screaming, opening his eyes wide: opening them wide, then, before a big toe.

*"Le gros orteil," excerpt from Oeuvres Complètes, Volume 1 by Georges Bataille.
© 1970, Editions Gallimard, Paris.

Georges Bataille, Visions of Excess: Selected Writings, 1927-1939, edited by Allan Stoekl, translated by Allan Stoekl, with Carl Lovitt and Donald Leslie, Jr. Theory and History of Literature, Volume 14, (University of Minnesota Press, 1985). English translation and introduction © 1985 by the University of Minnesota.

allowing the shod foot to be seen, jutting out from under a skirt, was regarded as indecent. Under no circumstances was it possible to touch the foot of a woman, this liberty being, with one exception, more grave than any other. Of course, the foot of the queen was the object of the most terrifying prohibition. Thus, according to Mme. D'Aulnoy, the Count of Villamediana, in love with Queen Elizabeth, had the idea of starting a fire in order to have the pleasure of carrying her in his arms.

"Almost the entire house, worth 100,000 écus, was burned, but he was consoled by the fact that, taking advantage of so favorable an occasion, he took the sovereign in his arms and carried her into a small staircase. He took some liberties there, and, something very much noticed in this country, he even touched her foot. A little page saw it, reported it to the king, and the latter had his revenge by killing the count with a pistol shot."

It is possible to see in these obsessions, as M. Reinach does, a progressive refinement of modesty that little by little has been able to reach the calf, the ankle, and the foot. This explanation, in part well founded, is however not sufficient if one wants to account for the hilarity commonly produced by simply imagining the toes. The play of fantasies and fears, of human necessities and aberrations, is in fact such that fingers have come to signify useful action and firm character; the toes stupor to base idiocy. The vicissitudes of organs, the profusion of stomachs, larynxes, and brains traversing innumerable animal, species, and individuals, carries the imagination along in an ebb and flow it does not willingly follow, due to a hatred of the still painfully perceptible frenzy of the bloody palpitations of the body. Man willingly imagines himself to be like the god Neptune, stilling his own waves with majesty; nevertheless, the bellowing waves of the viscera, in more or less incessant inflation and upheaval, brusquely put an end to his dignity. Blind but tranquil and strangely despising his obscure baseness, a given person, ready to call to mind the grandeurs of human history, as when his glance ascends a monument testifying to the grandeur of his nation, is stopped in mid-flight by an atrocious pain in his big toe because, though the most noble of animals, he nevertheless has corns on his feet; in other words, he has feet, and these feet independently lead an ignoble life.

Corns on the feet differ from headaches and toothaches by their baseness, and they are only laughable because of an ignominy explicable by the mud in which feet are found. Since by its physical attitude the human race distances itself as much as it can from terrestrial mud—one can imagine that a toe, always more or less damaged and humiliating, is psychologically analogous to the brutal fall of a man—in other words, to death. The hideously cadaverous and at the same time loud and proud appearance of the big toe corresponds to this deri-

allowing the shod foot to be seen, jutting out from under a skirt, was regarded as indecent. Under no circumstances was it possible to touch the foot of a women, this liberty being, with one exception, more grave than any other. Of course, the foot of the queen was the object of the most terrifying prohibition. Thus, according to Mme D'Aulnoy, the Count of Villamediana, in love with Queen Elizabeth, had the idea of starting a fire in order to have the pleasure of carrying her in his arms: "Almost the entire house, worth 100,000 écus, was burned, but he was consoled by the fact that, taking advantage of so favorable an occasion, he took the sovereign in his arms and carried her into a small staircase. He took some liberties there, and, something very much noticed in this country, he even touched her foot. A little page saw it, reported it to the king, and the latter had his revenge by killing the count with a pistol shot."

It is possible to see in these obsessions, as M. Reinach does, a progressive refinement of modesty that little by little has been able to reach the calf, the ankle, and the foot. This explanation, in part well founded, is however not sufficient if one wants to account for the hilarity commonly produced by simply imagining the *toes*. The play of fantasies and fears, of human necessities and aberrations, is in fact such that fingers have come to signify useful action and firm character, the toes stupor to base idiocy. The vicissitudes of organs, the profusion of stomachs, larynxes, and brains traversing innumerable animal, species, and individuals, carries the imagination along in an ebb and flow it does not willingly follow, due to a hatred of the still painfully perceptible frenzy of the bloody palpitations of the body. Man willingly imagines himself to be like the god Neptune, stilling his own waves with majesty; nevertheless, the bellowing waves of the viscera, in more or less incessant inflation and upheaval, brusquely put an end to his dignity. Blind, but tranquil and strangely despising his obscure baseness, a given person, ready to call to mind the grandeurs of human history, as when his glance ascends a monument testifying to the grandeur of his nation, is stopped in mid-flight by an atrocious pain in his big toe because, though the most noble of animals, he nevertheless has corns on his feet; in other words, he has feet, and these feet independently lead an ignoble life.

Corns on the feet differ from headaches and toothaches by their baseness, and they are only laughable because of an ignominy explicable by the mud in which feet are found. Since by its physical attitude the human race distances itself *as much as it can* from terrestrial mud—one can imagine that a toe, always more or less damaged and humiliating, is psychologically analogous to the brutal fall of a man—in other word, to death. The hideously cadaverous and at the same time loud and proud appearance of the big toe corresponds to this derision and gives a very shrill expression to the disorder of the human body, that product of the violent discord of the organs.

———————————

THE FORM OF THE BIG TOE is not, however, specifically monstrous: in this it is different than other parts of the body, the inside of a gaping mouth, for example. Only secondary (but common) deformations have been able to give its ignominy an exceptionally burlesque value. Now it is easy, most often, to account for burlesque values by means of extreme seductiveness. But we are led here to distinguish categorically two radically opposed kinds of seductiveness (whose habitual confusion entails the most absurd misunderstandings of language).

If a seductive element is to be attributed to the big toe, it is evidently not one to satisfy such exalted aspirations as, for example, the perfectly indelible taste that, in most cases, leads one to prefer elegant and correct forms. On the contrary, if one chooses, for example, the case of the Count of Villamediana, one can confirm that the pleasure he derived from touching the queen's foot specifically derived from the ugliness and infection represented by the *baseness* of the foot, in practice by most deformed feet. Thus, supposing that the queen's foot was perfectly pretty, it still derived its sacrilegious charm from deformed and muddy feet. Since a queen is *a priori* a more *ideal* and ethereal being than any other, it was human to the point of laceration to touch what in fact was not very different from the stinking foot of a thug. Here one submits to a seduction radically opposed to that caused by light and ideal beauty; the two orders of seduction are often confused because a person constantly moves from one to the other, and, given this back and forth movement, whether it finds its ends in one direction or the other, seduction is all the more acute when the movement is more brutal.

As for the big toe, classic foot fetishism leading to the licking of toes categorically indicates that it is a phenomenon of base seduction, which accounts for the burlesque value that is always more or less attached to the pleasures condemned by pure and superficial men.

———————————

THE MEANING OF THIS ARTICLE lies in its insistence on a direct and explicit questioning of seductiveness, without taking into account poetic concoctions that are, ultimately, nothing but a diversion (most human beings are naturally feeble and can only abandon themselves to their instincts when in a poetic haze). A return to reality does not imply any new acceptances, but means that one is seduced in a base manner, without transpositions and to the point of screaming, opening his eyes wide: opening them wide, then, before a big toe.

"Le gros orteil" excerpt from *Oeuvres Complètes, Volume I* by Georges Bataille. © 1970, Editions Gallimard, Paris.

Georges Bataille, *Visions of Excess: Selected Writings, 1927-1939*, edited by Allan Stoekl, translated by Allan Stoekl, with Carl Lovitt and Donald Leslie, Jr. *Theory and History of Literature*, Volume 14. (University of Minnesota Press, 1985). English translation and introduction © 1985 by the University of Minnesota.

FEET — WITHOUT FETISH —

ROSALIND KRAUSS

Georges Bataille's "Big Toe" joins the *Documents* "Dictionary" project as yet another body part—the eye, the mouth—to which an essay is devoted. And as with the others, the very choice to focus on the individual organ, suggesting its detachment from the rest of the human body, could be instantly read as a psychoanalytic move, invoking fetishism. No matter how repulsive the big toe might be—how dirty, calloused, deformed by bunions, corns, cracked nails, and the like—it is presented as having a powerful sexual attraction. This might make it easy to assume that the mechanics of such an attraction run through the channels of the fetish's logic of substitution. The shock of the "absent" (read castrated) phallus is unconsciously re-equilibrated by putting a proxy in its place: underwear, shoes, nose, foot...why not toe?

In his essay on Bataille's text, Roland Barthes says why not.[1] Psychoanalysis would plot the body's meaning along the "natural" axis of $\frac{mouth}{anus}$, thereby producing a paradigm of inbuilt oppositions. The narrative this yields is one of libidinal development, oral drives ceding to anal ones, themselves ceding to phallic. It is in the light of this narrative that the fetish-as-substitute is born. But Bataille's position is that the meaning organizing the body is not "natural." It is instead the result of an imposition of values, specifically human values such as nobility or loftiness, to which the opposite conditions of ignobility or lowness set the terms of the structural paradigm: $\frac{noble}{ignoble}$; $\frac{high}{low}$. In this sense, if Bataille begins by saying that the toe is the most human part of the body, it is not just due to the opposition $\frac{hand}{foot}$ —with the loss of the prehensile character of the toe changing man from

1. Roland Barthes, "Outcomes of the Text" (1973), The Rustle of Language, trans. Richard Howard (New York: Hill & Wang, 1986).

33

ROSALIND KRAUSS

Georges Bataille's "Big Toe" joins the Documents "Dictionary" project as yet another body part—the eye, the mouth—to which an essay is devoted. And as with the others, the very choice to focus on the individual organ, suggesting its detachment from the rest of the human body, could be instantly read as a psychoanalytic move, invoking fetishism. No matter how repulsive the big toe might be—how dirty, calloused, deformed by bunions, corns, cracked nails, and the like—it is presented as having a powerful sexual attraction. This might make it easy to assume that the mechanics of such an attraction run through the channels of the fetish's logic of substitution. The shock of the "absent" (read castrated) phallus is unconsciously re-equilibrated by putting a proxy in its place: underwear, shoes, nose, foot...why not toe?

In his essay on Bataille's text, Roland Barthes says why not[1]. Psychoanalysis would plot the body's meaning along the "natural" axis of $\frac{\text{mouth}}{\text{anus}}$, thereby producing a paradigm of inbuilt oppositions. The narrative this yields is one of libidinal development, oral drives ceding to anal ones, themselves ceding to phallic. It is in the light of this narrative that the fetish-as-substitute is born. But Bataille's position is that the meaning organizing the body is not "natural". It is instead the result of an imposition of values, specifically human values such as nobility or loftiness, to which the opposite conditions of ignobility or lowness set the terms of the structural paradigm: $\frac{\text{noble}}{\text{ignoble}} : \frac{\text{high}}{\text{low}}$. In this sense, it Bataille begins by saying that the toe is the most human part of the body, it is not just due to the opposition $\frac{\text{hand}}{\text{foot}}$ —with the loss of the prehensile character of the toe of changing man from

1. Roland Barthes, "Outcomes of the Text," Richard Howard (New York: Hill & Wang, 1986).

ape, by forcing him into the condition of the erect biped (no more hanging from trees)—which anatomically raises man above his more bestial ancestors. Rather, it is due to the institution of high and low as values that compellingly revector the body, so that $\frac{\text{oral}}{\text{anal}}$ is supplanted by $\frac{\text{toe}}{\text{crown-of-head}}$ and the body itself is seen to found the human meaning of the choice between nobility and its opposite: feet in the mud but head in the clouds.

This opposition, however, joins apples and oranges, in that the idealist values of the $\frac{\text{noble}}{\text{ignoble}}$ couple are now yoked to the aggressive materialism of the "low." Barthes pulls synonyms for these terms from other Bataille texts. There "noble" is connected with generosity and splendor; "ignoble" with hypocrisy and shame; but "low" with spittle, mud, streaming blood, the cadaver in decomposition—all of these being types of matter rather than ethical terms. The result of this yoking is that the (structuralist) paradigm which operates meaning changes from binary— $\frac{\text{noble}}{\text{ignoble}}$ —to ternary: $\frac{\text{noble}}{\frac{\text{ignoble}}{\text{low}}}$. Normally, there is nothing unusual about this—a third term added to a structural binary continues its logic either by adding its terms together (both/and)— $\frac{\text{green light}}{\text{red light}}$ + yellow light—or by producing the "neutral" status of neither/nor: The gendered pair man ǀ woman "neutralized" by the universal condition of "humanity." But "low" does not add on logically to $\frac{\text{noble}}{\text{ignoble}}$; it infects the noble with a kind of base materiality as it is in turn infected with a non-material ethos. To infect matter is to deny it an in-itself, a notion of it as pure. Matter is thus split from within, not because it is taken up within the form of a proxy—a fetish— and thus given the meaning of the substitute; but because in its very brutishness it is opened to value, to an appeal for someone, becoming in this way seductive. The fetish, we could say, operates according to rule, whether psychoanalytic or ritualistic. But Bataille's concept of the lowness of the big toe is that it confronts us with what Barthes calls "an independent, eccentric, irreducible term—

seduction outside the (structural)

law." It seduces us basely without

the comfort of Oedipus as companion

and excuse.

Rosalind E. Krauss co-curated the exhibition "L'Inform: mode d'emploi" (Centre Pompidou, Paris, Summer 1996) with Yve-Alain Bois. Their catalogue, *Formless: A User's Guide,* will be issued by Zone Books this fall.

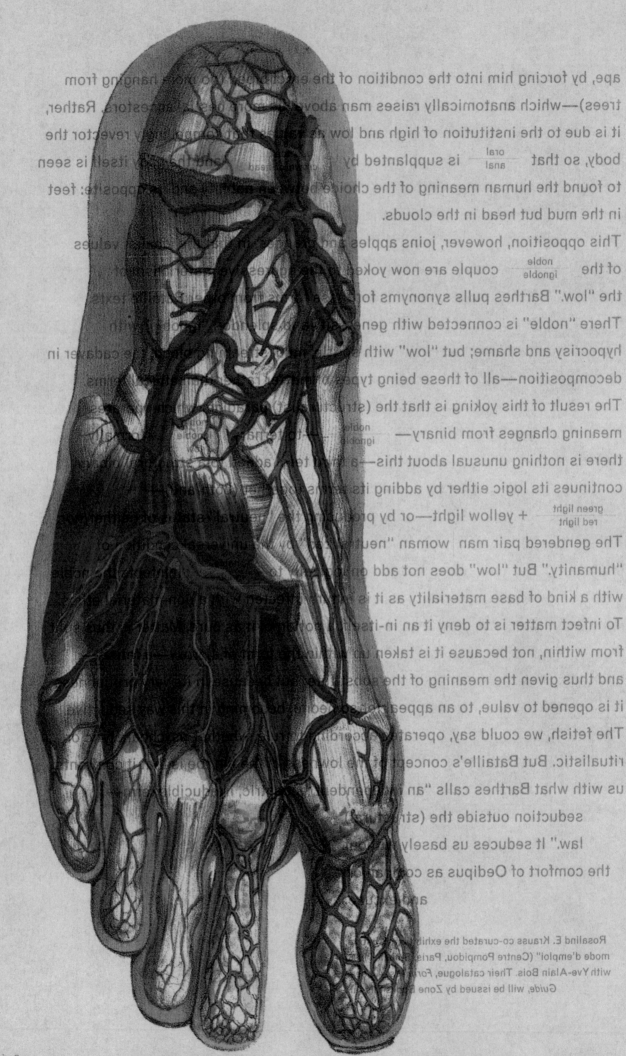

ape, by forcing him into the condition of the ... to trees hanging from trees)—which anatomically raises man above ... ancestors. Rather, it is due to the institution of high and low ... reverses for the body, so that $\frac{oral}{anal}$ is supplanted by ... head ... and the body itself is seen to found the human meaning of the choice between noble and composite: feet in the mud but head in the clouds.

This opposition, however, joins apples and ... values of the noble/ignoble couple are now yoked ... the "low." Barthes pulls synonyms for ... There "noble" is connected with gen... hypocrisy and shame; but "low" with ... decomposition—all of these being types o... The result of this yoking is that the (str... meaning changes from binary— noble/ignoble ... there is nothing unusual about this— ... continues its logic either by adding its ... green light / red light + yellow light—or by pro... The gendered pair man woman "neut... "humanity." But "low" does not add a... with a kind of base materiality as it is... To infect matter is to deny it an in-itse... from within, not because it is taken up ... and thus given the meaning of the subs... it is opened to value, to an appea... The fetish, we could say, operat... ritualistic. But Bataille's concept i... us with what Barthes calls "an... seduction outside the (str... law." It seduces us basely... the comfort of Oedipus as co...

Rosalind E. Krauss co-curated the exhib... mode d'emploi." (Centre Pompidou, Paris... with Yve-Alain Bois. Their catalogue, For... Guide, will be issued by Zone b...

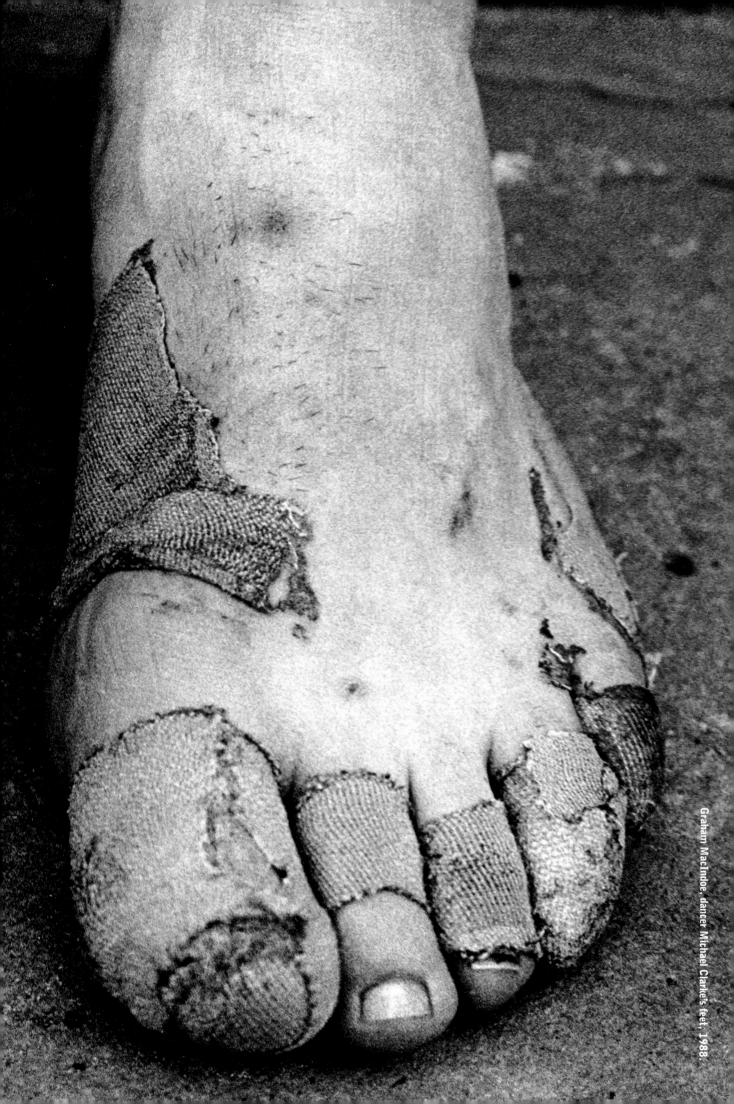

André Kertész, *Buy*, New York, 1962. Courtesy of
and © The Estate of André Kertész.

Martin Munkacsi, *The Sidewalks of Rio de Janeiro, Brazil*, ca. 1932. © Joan Munkacsi. Courtesy of Howard Greenberg Gallery, NYC.

Marc Riboud, *Children Running on a Country Road*, 1962. © Marc Riboud/Magnum Photos.

Footnotes

This index lists some
resources for the study
of feet and shoes.

Northampton Museum
Guildhall Road
Northampton
NN1 1DP
England
Keeper of the Boot and Shoe
Collection: Ms. Victoria Wood
Tel: (44) 1.604.233.500 ext.5115
Fax: (44) 1.604.238.720

Clarks' Shoe Museum
High Street
Street, Somerset
BA16 OYA
England
Contact: Mrs. Jean Brook

Deutsches Leder und
Schuhmuseum
Frankfurterstrasse 86
Offenbach am Main
D-PLZ 63067 Germany
Director: Dr. Renate
Wente-Lukas

Schuhmuseum
19 Dinkelbachstrasse
678 Pirmisens
Germany

Stadt Museum
Schloss
485 Weissenfels
Germany

Schumuseum (sports)
Adidas
Herzogenaurach
Germany

Musée de la Chaussure
Ancien Couvent de la
Visitation
2 Rue St. Marie
26100 Romans-sur-Izere,
Drome, France
Curator: Mlle. Marie-Joseph
Bossan

Fax: 75.02.97.26
Musée de la Chausseur
La Tour Raoul, Le Chateau
Foureres
Ile-et-Vilaine, France

Nederlands Schoenen &
Lederwaren Museum
Elzenweg 25
5144 MB Waalijk
Netherlands
Curator: Dr. Wim Blok

National Schoeiselmuseum
Wijngaardstraat 9
8700 Izegem
Belgium
Conservator: Roger Bekaert
Sint. Crispijnstrasse 27,
8700 Izegem

Bally Schuhmuseum
Felsgarten
CH 5012 Schoenward
Switzerland
Curator: Ms. Karin Baumann
Puntener
Tel: (062) 858 20 62

Museo del Calzado Antiguo,
Casa de S. Felipe Neri
Barcelona 2, Spain
Hon. Curator: Senior M. Arnal

Museo Salvatore Ferragamo
Palazzo Spini Feroni
Via dei Tornabuoni 2
50123 Firenze, Italy
Curator: Stefania Ricci
By appointment.
Tel: (39)(55)3360.546

Civico Museo della Calzatura
Palazzo Crespi
Vigevano, Italy

Obuvnicke Muszeum Svit Zlin
Czech Republic
Director: Hana Kozlovska

Bata Shoe Museum
327 Bloor Street West
Toronto, Ontario
M5S 1W7 Canada
Director: Edward Maeder,
Curator: Jonathon Walford
Tel: (416) 979.7799
Fax: (416) 979.0088

'El Borcequi' Shoe Museum
Bolivar 27
Colonia Centro, C.P.
06000 Mexico D.F.
Curator: Carmen Artigas

Japanese Footwear Museum
Matsunaga, Fukuyama
Hiroshima, Japan
Director: Mr. Shigeo
Maruyama

China Shoe Museum
P.O. Box 081-926
200081 Shangai
P.R. China
Director: Mr. Luo Chong-Qui

The Metropolitan
Museum of Art
Fifth Avenue at
82nd Street
New York, New York 10028
The Costume Institute
Tel: (212) 535.7710

The Museum at The Fashion
Institute of Technology
Seventh Avenue at 27th Street
New York, New York 10001
Tel: (212) 760.7708

The Brooklyn Museum
200 Eastern Parkway
Brooklyn, New York 11238
Department of Costumes
and Textiles
Curator: Patricia Mears
Tel: (718) 638.5000
Fax: (718) 638.3731

The Glenn Roberts Collection
301 East 48th Street #4A
New York, New York 10017
Tel/Fax: (212) 759.8127
The largest collection outside
Asia of women's Chinese
Lotus shoes, or shoes for
bound feet.

The Burns Collection, Ltd.
140 East 38th Street
New York, New York 10016
Tel: (212) 889.1938
Fax: (212) 481.9113
Web: www.burnsarchive.com
The Burns Collection
contains medical
photographs including
documents that pertain to
orthopedics.

The Connecticut Historical
Society
1 Elizabeth Street
at Asylum Avenue
Hartford, CT 06105
Curatorial Assistant:
Daniel Trucke,
Tel: (860) 236.5621 x245
Fax: (860) 236.2664
The Connecticut Historical
Society shoe collection
includes more than 600 items,
dating from the 17th century
through the late 20th century,
including a noteworthy
assortment of rubber
footwear, much of it made in
Connecticut, which was an
early center of rubber
production.

Lynn Historical Society
125 Green Street
Lynn, MA 01902
Director: Ken Turino
Tel: (617) 592.2465
Fax: (617) 592.0012
Founded in 1897, the
collections at the society
consist of a library and an
artifact collection. In the 19th
century, Lynn was one of the
largest centers of shoe
manufacturing. The society
has a fine collection of over
1500 pieces of shoemaking
equipment, over 400 shoes,
plus a fully out-fitted "10-
footer" shop.

The Peabody Essex Museum
East India Square
Salem, MA 01970
Registrar: Paula Richter
Tel: (508) 745.1876 ext.3156;
(800) 745.4054
Fax: (508) 740.3617
Web: www.pem.org
E-mail: pem@pem.org
The footwear collection of the
Peabody Essex Museum
includes approximately 4000
examples from around the
world spanning several
centuries. The museum's
Phillips libraries hold more
than two million books,
manuscripts, including
documentary materials
related to the shoe-making
industry in Massachusetts.

Center for the History of Foot
Care & Foot Wear
Pennsylvania College of
Podiatric Medicine
8th at Race Street
Philadelphia, PA 19107
Director: Barbara Williams
Tel: (215) 625.5243
The primary interest of the
Center is in the profession of
podiatry: its origins and
development; its
personalities, its institutions,
and its literature. The center
collects related archival
material and artifacts. A
secondary interest pertains to
the foot itself: its origins as
well as its representation in
art and literature. In addition,
the center examines the
history and social
significance of shoes and
shoemakers, primarily
through exhibitions. Among
its holdings are 18th and 19th
century shoe collections as
well as a collection of
celebrity shoes, including
those of many First Ladies
and sports figures such as
Joe Frazier.

Dr. John N. Bergmann DPM,
FACPP
1860 John's Drive
Glenview, IL 60025
Tel: (847) 729.7923
Fax: (847) 729.7945
Web: johnortho@aol.com
Podiatrist specializing in
orthotics for control of foot
conditions caused by
abnormal biomechanics.
Dr. Bergmann also directs the
Bergmann Orthotic Lab, Inc.
which specializes in 3-
dimensional imaging of the
foot with the Bergmann
Optical Laser Foot Scanner.

Dr. William M. Scholl College
of Podiatric Medicine
1001 North Dearborn Street
Chicago, IL 60610
Director of Public Relations:
Dominic Calabrese
Tel: (312) 280.2850
Fax: (312) 280.2997
Founded in 1912, Scholl
College is one of only seven
colleges of Podiatric medicine
in the U.S. "Feet First: The Dr.
Scholl Story" is a permanent
exhibition housed at the
school and features a wealth
of historical photos and
artifacts.

Boston Dynamics, Inc.
614 Massachusetts Avenue,
Cambridge, MA 02139
Contact: Marc Raibert,
Director
Tel: (617) 621.2929
Fax: (617) 621.1606
Web: www.bdi.com
Boston Dynamics Inc (BDI)
creates automated computer
characters and engineering
simulations for things that
move, such as humans,
animals, robots, and
electromechanical devices.
Each simulation is coupled to
3D computer graphics that
animate the simulated
behavior. Its technical staff
includes engineers and
scientists whose strengths
are in computer science and
engineering, robotics, and
biomechanics.

The Poly-PEDAL Laboratory
Department of Integrative
Biology
Valley Life Science Building
University of California at
Berkeley
Berkeley, CA 94720
Director: Robert Full
Tel: (510) 642.9896
Fax: (510) 643.6264
Web:
www.polypedal.berkeley.edu
The Poly-PEDAL Laboratory
(Performance, Energetics
and Dynamics of Animal
Locomotion) studies the
motion of many-legged
animals, everything from
crabs and cockroaches to
scorpians, centipedes, lizards
and frogs. They seek general
architectural principles for
species which have evolved
vastly different solutions to
the problem of terrestrial
locomotion using feet.

MODERN DANCE BEGAN

when choreographers kicked off their ballet slippers and danced BAREFOOT on stage.
Along with their footwear, these early pioneers—such as Loie Fuller and Isadora Duncan—also abandoned the pointed toe as the standard measure of a dancer's movement, and in so doing cleared the slate for an entirely new vocabulary of twentieth century dance. By the 1940s, Martha Graham had created an elaborate language of highly expressive movement that depended on bare feet planted squarely on solid ground, and a decade later, Graham's student Merce Cunningham, focused his search for new movement on walking. Working with university students in 1952, Cunningham suggested that they begin with ordinary gestures—"These were accepted as movement in daily life, why not on stage?" he wrote—and he used the idionsyncratic pedestrian styles of each of them as the foundation for his choreographic design.

For dancers in the post-Cunningham era—from the early-sixties on—walking became the common denominator that linked their innovative experiments. Among the choreographers who formed The Judson Dance Theater in 1962, including Yvonne Rainer, Trisha Brown, Steve Paxton and Lucinda Childs, walking represented a radical stance against the dance establishment. It was a way of refuting the exclusivity of western dance forms and the suppression of individuality which its standards demanded. It was a way of democratizing dance, of insisting that anyone could be a dancer—"I envisioned myself

WALK

RoseLee Goldberg

as a post-modern dance evangelist bringing movement to the masses," Rainer wrote. And it was also a means for dance to serve as an accessible vehicle for social commentary, which by the late 1960s included reference to the tensions and nationwide anger provoked by the Vietnam War.

Dancers in the 1970s worked hard at making their movements look as natural and as close to everyday activities as possible. At the same time they attempted to foreground the process of art-making, often commenting on the mechanics of a particular movement as they danced. Their efforts paralleled the work of many conceptual artists of the period—Vito Acconci, Dennis Oppenheim, and Sol Le Witt among others—for whom the idea of art was as important as the actual execution of a work. Dance was used to investigate the meaning of the

BY THE AFFLUENT 80s,
WALKING
HAD EVOLVED INTO A
STRUT.
DANCERS
FLAUNTED
THEIR EMANCIPATION
ON A STAGE

BEREFT OF MEN.

THE DANCERS'
BARE LEGS
SEEMED TO BE
ANATOMICAL EXTENSION
OF THEIR
**BARBIE DOLL–STYLE
PUMPS**

form itself, and this highly conceptual approach erupted in a broad range of radical and compelling proposals. Trisha Brown devised a series of what she called equipment pieces to illustrate that dance is, in essence, a matter of gravity. In *Walking on the Wall* (1971), her dancers literally walked along the walls of a gallery, suspended from the ceiling by mountaineering equipment. Lucinda Childs used intricate notation to determine the paths her dancers would take, even as they increased the speed of their walking to the point at which they became airborne in a flurry of leaps and turns. Laura Dean, working from rigorous drawings that included an elaborate counting system, introduced a distinctive rhythm into her walk; performers stamped their feet unevenly, causing her modern dancers to spin in circles like ancient whirling dervishes. Dana Reitz, on the other hand, walked so slowly that watching her cross a stage was like viewing a series of Muybridge stills, where detecting changes in skeletal structure through repetition became the fascinating appeal of her work.

By the affluent 1980s, walking had evolved into a far more ambitious strut. The European walk, languorous and steep-heeled, distinguished the choreography of dancers on the eastern side of the Atlantic from their American counterparts. Pina Bausch's long-limbed dancers combined the edgy appeal of the streetwalker with the forceful precision of the highly trained dancer; with each step they reintroduced a narrative thread into modern dance, creating, with their tautly configured strolling, vital ballets of longing and tenderness between male and female performers. Anne Teresa de Keersmaeker upped the

DANC

ante between the sexes, with a troupe of young female dancers who flaunted their emancipation on a stage bereft of men. The dancers' bare legs seemed to be anatomical extensions of their Barbie Doll–style pumps; despite the ridiculous arches of those shoes, they hit the ground running with fast-paced kicks and tumbles.

Such streetwalking could not be more different from the urban rhythms of America's streets and avenues. According to Jawole Willa Jo Zollar, of Urban Bush Women, "This country is more Africanized than we realize." Noting the subtle effects of African-American movement on the population at large—from tap and rock to double dutch and break dancing—Urban Bush Women created a series of ballets which incorporated the company's extensive research into African-American traditions. The 'shout dance,' which involves dancers shuffling in a circle, actually dates back to sacred African ritual. Jane Comfort, on the other hand, compiled a repertoire of movements that reflected gender roles and specific ethnicities, which through repetition and rhythm became energetic and fluid dance. "Why do men always take up so much room?" "Why can't I spread my legs?" a female voice repeatedly asked over a sound track of rap rhythms, in a work where dancers seated themselves in a long row as though on an attached bench in a subway car. Moving through a pattern of positions uncannily familiar to any rider—the men leaning back, legs apart, and arms clasped behind their heads with elbows extended like bulls' horns from their shoulders, while the women wove their legs and arms together until their bodies looked like folded paper fans—Comfort created an exotic choreography from the colloquialisms of everyday body-language.

Having begun this walking tour, one is tempted to take off on quite another path, down the trail through art history. After all, landscape painting of the last century captured not only the beauty of the natural setting, but also the meandering route that took the artist there in the first place. More recently, the sculptor Richard Long made an art of it, walking on remote hilltops or across distant deserts, insisting all the while that his gallery exhibitions were mere detours from the splendors of actual physical landscapes. Performance artists Marina Abramovic and Ulay made a spectacular thousand-mile walk across the Great Wall of China in 1988; planned as a demonstration of will, and as a giant step across continents of varied cultures into the Chinese hinterland, their journey was also a remarkable dissertation on the art of walking.

In dance, performance, and the visual arts, walking heightens our perception of walking as a day-to-day experience, and points to our fallibility too. Laurie Anderson, in a song from *United States*, called "Looking for You; Walking and Falling," captures its essence: "You're walking. And you don't always realize it, but you're always falling....Over and over, you're falling. And then catching yourself from falling. And this is how you can be walking and falling at the same time."

RoseLee Goldberg, art historian, critic and curator, teaches at New York University and is a frequent contributor to *Artforum*.

FALL

ING

ARCH RIVALS

LINDA O'KEEFFE

Fetish Shoes, Designer
unknown, 1973-1975,
Mexico. Collection of The
Museum of the Fashion
Institute of Technology,
New York. Photograph
by Jay Zukerkorn.

SINCE TIME IMMEMORIAL, HEELED OR PLATFORMED SHOES
HAVE ELEVATED WOMEN AND EMPOWERED US BY EXTENDING
OUR REACH, BUT THEY HAVE ALSO CLIPPED OUR WINGS,
INHIBITED OUR WALK AND RESTRICTED OUR INDEPENDENCE.
Fetish footwear exemplifies this curious dynamic with its staggeringly high
heels that allow a woman the choice to either dominate her partner or to
become the object of his desire.

But men never intended to either subjugate or glorify women when they first designed high shoes: Their goals were more mundane. In Mesopotamia, butchers constructed stilt-like overshoes so they could maneuver on carcass-strewn floors. Later, nomadic horsemen built up the back sole of their boots to grip their stirrups more effectively.

The first enduring fashion in platformed shoes originated in the 15th century when Venetian husbands schemed to ground their gadding wives by popularizing the footstool-like sandals worn by the sequestered beauties in Turkish harems. The Italian wives had the wit to coax their shoemakers into substituting wooden soles with platforms made of cork, and the chopine, "the shoe for important women," was born.

Before regulations were imposed, women mounted themselves on chopines that were a full yard high. Upholstered in rich velvets and studded with pearls and precious gems, the style remained popular for two centuries, during which tourists flocked to Italy to gawk at the giantesses who peered down onto the masses like living statues. Up on their chopines, women appeared serene when stationary, but their gait was awkward and ungainly. To stabilize themselves, they held their bodies stiffly, lumbering and lurching with the support of two servants acting as human crutches. Even then they only managed to inch along "at prisoner's pace." Men realized that such highly visible wives had little opportunity to be unfaithful, and women enjoyed the exhibitionistic potential of the shoes. They were content to return home, dismount, and step down into the mortal world.

Five centuries earlier, Chinese men had developed an almost irreversible method of immobilizing their wives. The feet of 5- or 6-year-old girls' feet were permanently bandaged in the hope they would develop into three inch-long Golden Lotus feet, a rare attribute for women. These women were revered by society, respected for their passivity, and regarded as the epitome of femininity. Men marveled at the daintiness of their wives' bound feet, and their intricately embroidered shoes drove them wild with lust, partly because they believed stunting the feet sensitized the rest of a woman's body and left her permanently primed for sex.

When reclining in a daybed or in a sedan, the perfumed, ornamented women resembled rare prizes, but when they walked without the help of a cane or a servant's arm, they quickly lost their balance and had to waddle and flail their arms like a duck. Lotus shoes with wedged heels turned walking into an even more painful ordeal. The custom endured for more than a thousand years: Without small feet women had little or no chance of marrying well.

Catherine de Medici introduced one-inch heeled shoes to the French court in the mid-16th century, and by the time Louis XIV adopted the style a century later, he proclaimed red heels a sign of nobility. By the middle of the 18th century, when nonfunctional clothing and footwear were marks of gentility, women could be seen teetering on heels up to 6 inches high. These distant relatives of the stiletto were excruciating to walk in because they thrust the weight of the body onto the toes. Women adopted a semi-crouching stance and canes became a fashionable necessity.

But discomfort and artifice go hand in hand. At that time, women laced their corsets so tightly that their ribs overlapped; their

James Arpad, Shoe, circa 1939,
New York. Silk satin, wood, leather.
Courtesy of The Brooklyn Museum,
x1025.2a. The Brooklyn Museum
Collection.

James Arpad, Shoe, circa 1939.
Silk satin, wood, leather. Courtesy
of The Brooklyn Museum, x1025.1a.
The Brooklyn Museum Collection.

hooped skirts, often 8 feet in diameter, puffed out like hot-air balloons and ritualized the simple act of passing through a doorway. Their extraordinarily tall wigs—showcases for cages of live birds or replicas of ships at full sail—forced them on their knees when traveling by coach. Casanova captured the absurdity of society's affectations in his memoirs when he described a woman in haste hitching up her crinoline in order to "hop like a kangaroo."

Heeled shoes disguised flat feet which, beginning in the 17th century, were considered vulgar. Dropped arches and widely spread feet characterized the working classes, so monied men and women achieved instant aristocratic-looking arches when they slipped on a pair of high heels.

Another reason heels were popular—and still are—is because they foreshorten the foot. There are more than 500 versions of the Cinderella story (the earliest dates back to Egyptian times), so it is safe to assume that little girls throughout the world are spoon-fed the notion that femininity and sexual passivity are engendered in a dainty, delicate foot. Some hold the fairy tale responsible for the custom of Chinese footbinding, which was banned as recently as the 1930s. Some hold the scullery maid responsible for the fact that a majority of women still insist on buying shoes that are, on average, one size too small for them.

Discomfort and artifice go hand in hand: when nonfunctional shoes were marks of gentility, women could be seen teetering on heels up to 6 inches high.

The stiletto is undoubtedly the most controversial shoe of this century. Banned from public buildings, campaigned against, stilettos even forced the development of floor coverings strong enough to resist being pock marked by sharp heel tips. In the 1950s the stiletto's popularity was sometimes attributed to the fact that it held the foot at an angle that caused the buttocks to undulate twice as much as they would in flat shoes, transmitting sexual sensations throughout the body. That same placement of the foot, according to Kinsey, mimicked the position both feet adopt during sexual arousal when the toes extend and adopt an *en pointe* alignment with the leg. He compared it to the "courtship strut" anthropologists had already documented in the animal kingdom.

High heels are still provocative. Some feminists continue to see them as symbols of the male objectification of women, while others —like Camille Paglia—claim them as their own. A former advocate of militant lesbianism who all but outlawed skirts during the 1960s, Paglia admits to currently feeling "more powerful in sexual clothing, in erotic clothing. That is, I enjoy wearing cosmetics now, I enjoy wearing high heels."

Heels certainly make a woman's body appear taut and toned, and some women feel empowered when they wear them—they attribute that feeling to a change in their anatomy. In heels, a woman's breasts and buttocks protrude forward and up, her spine elongates, her lower back arches, her leg line lengthens, her calf appears to be more muscular and her ankle seems slimmer. Suddenly she is looking down on men she formerly looked up to. It is not possible to cower in high heels. But neither, say detractors, is it possible to run.

Then there is Tina Turner.

LINDA O'KEEFFE is a Senior Editor at *Metropolitan Home,* and the author of *Shoes*, published this year by Workman.

SUSAN BENNIS:
High heels have never gone out of fashion.
Men love they way they look on a woman's legs because of what
they do: The muscle in the leg is pulled taut, so the shape of the
leg is elongated and it makes you look slimmer.
The leg looks much prettier, more appealing,
much more sexual, I suppose.
A beautiful pair of high-heeled shoes can transform even
women whose legs are not very attractive.
High heels pull the muscles up and
give a nicer shape to the leg.
For women who do have beautiful legs,
heels make them even more so.

A woman who can walk elegantly
in a high-heeled shoe is almost majestic.
It's a different, more powerful feeling
when your body is up on heels.
Physically, we aren't meant to be up on five-inch heels,
so we've tried to develop heels that are comfortable:
we have padding on the inside, we've put
extra cushioning where the ball of the foot is.
These technical things make them more
comfortable, more inviting to put on.

Susan Bennis and Warren Edwards,
Mood Swings (shoes), Fall 1995.
Photographed by Jay Zukerkorn.

WARREN
EDWARDS:
When we started out,
people were tottering
around on very high
platforms. We never got
involved with any of that
stuff. We went off and
did a whole different look,
a much more refined
1940s look. And it was right
at the time, too. It could
have been wrong. It's not really
a science; it's all a bit of a chance.

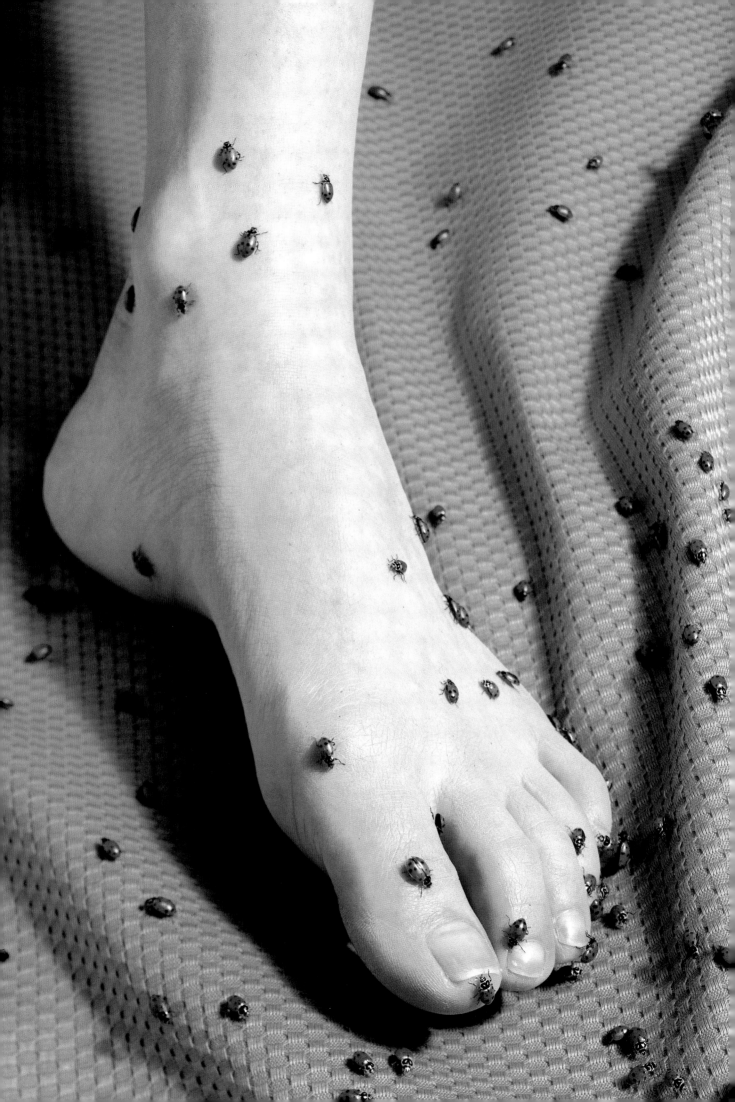

The
marvelous
thing
about
asking
the
designer
GEOFFREY BEENE
a
question—
any
question—
is
that
his
answer
is
never
what
you
expect.
(The
same
rule
applies
to
his
clothing.)
When
asked
why
so
many
of
his
models
are
shown
barefoot,
he
offered
some
suggestions,
but
ultimately
preferred
to talk
about
ears.

I sent a girl out on
the runway barefoot
was in the 1980s. Her
shoes didn't arrive on
time and she couldn't
fit in anything else
we had around. So I
finally said to her,
"Listen, chuck it. Don't
wear anything. Go out
there barefoot."
And it worked.

It's not the idea
of being barefoot
that appeals to me.
Its the idea
of the void—the
idea that there
is nothing to
distract you from
what you're
supposed to see,
which is the
clothes. It takes
a lot of time to
perfect the right
shoe. When
you have no
shoes
you have no
problems.
Also, I like
the way a
woman
moves
barefoot.

PHOTOGRAPHS BY
ANDREW ECCLES FOR
GEOFFREY BEENE

For years I thought
the foot was the ugliest part of the body. Now I'm not quite so sure
because the ear is edging in. You spend as much time
as I do sitting in airports, looking at people,
and you see a lot of ears, believe me.

CALL ME IMELDA.

I don't have thousands of pairs of shoes,

some duplicates, some the same style in different colors. I do, however, have 26 pairs of black shoes, one pair in duplicate (would there were others!), some the same style in different fabrics. These duplicates allow us—Mrs. Marcos and me—to wear our favorites without fear of rain, nor sleet, nor scuffs, nor hail. And if, by some strange chance, an evening slipper is left behind on the palace steps at the stroke of midnight, there is another to replace it back at home. I dare say our collections, however different in scale, serve the same purpose. Shoes are our gold, our garlic, our bells, our books, and our candles, and we shore them against our ruin. We adore shoes, and we believe in their powers (second only to the powers of chocolate).

We are sole sisters. We know that if Achilles had been wearing ghillies, he would be alive today. We understand the true moral of Cinderella: The girl with the best shoes gets the best life.

Some of us, mostly female, are born knowing this, and find our knowledge mirrored in fairy tales, each appropriate to its time and place, all variants on the same theme. I think the American Cinderella is actually Dorothy, the Judy Garland character in the MGM *The Wizard of Oz* (1939), who is somewhat older than the little girl of the L. Frank Baum original (1899), and has sexier shoes. For although you cannot imagine the girl in the gingham dress clicking any other heels together three times, her ruby slippers are the quite understandable invention of filmmakers more interested in Technicolor than literary authenticity. (Red shoes are a whole subject onto themselves—women either love them or hate them, and they are either good, like Dorothy's, or bad, like the ones Moira Shearer gets stuck in, in the awful ballerina movie called, of course, *The Red Shoes* (1948).)

In the original—that is the book, which is itself quite charming—even if its lion is no match for Bert Lahr (but then, who is?)—Dorothy's slippers are silver, and they attract not a prince, but the Wicked Witch of the West, who enslaves the innocent child:

> *Dorothy followed her through many of the beautiful rooms in her castle until they came to the kitchen, where the Witch made her clean the pots and kettles and sweep the floor and keep the fire fed with wood.*

> *The Wonderful Wizard of Oz*, L. Frank Baum, 1899, Geo. M. Hill Co., Chicago, New York, p. 150.

Willie Cole, *Made in the Phillipines II,* **1993.**
Shoes, PVC pipe, wood, and wheels; 39 x 44 x 44 1/2 in.
Collection of Eileen and Peter Norton. Courtesy of Alexander and Bonin Gallery, New York.
Photo: D. James Dee.

This girl with the broom is unmistakably Cinderella, or at least *a* Cinderella, one of hundreds, if not thousands. (In 1893, an Englishwoman named Marian R. Cox published a useful volume called *Cinderella Three Hundred and Forty-Five Variants.*) The glass slippers—the invention of the Frenchman Perrault, who upgraded them from fur-lined flats—are the tip of the iceberg.

Going beneath the surface, in 1975 the Austrian-born child psychologist Dr. Bruno Bettelheim published a generally quite readable book called *The Uses of Enchantment.* A lot of it is hair curling, particularly the Freudian bits. (Somehow the Jungians are more soothing.) The good doctor handily explicates his way through *The Three Little Pigs, Hansel and Gretel, Little Red Riding Hood, Jack and the Beanstalk, Snow White, Goldilocks,* and *Sleeping Beauty,* until, on page 236, he comes to *Cinderella.* It trips him up completely.

For the next 40 pages, we read about sibling rivalry, clandestine actions, primary narcissism, toilet training, Oedipal guilt and rejection, vestal virgins, the ritual meaning of ashes, the rejection of paganism, and so forth, hoping that soon we will get to the shoe part. But when at last we do—yuck! Bettelheim's "symbolic meanings for the fitting of the precious slipper onto the appropriate foot" are not the kinds of things you think about when you slide into your scuffs—that is unless you always think about penis envy and castration anxiety before you have had your morning coffee, as quite possibly Dr. Bettelheim did.

At any rate, it is somewhere during this part of his pursuit (which is beginning to resemble the prince's search for Cinderella in Act III Scene II of the Russian ballet versions of the story, an episode sometimes referred to as "Around the World") that the psychoanalyst inadvertently reveals something quite telling about his own understanding—or lack thereof—of women and shoes. He writes: "A very strange incident which takes place in most versions of 'Cinderella' is the stepsisters mutilation of their feet to make them fit the slipper." Strange?!? I guess Mrs. Bettelheim did not wear Manolo Blahniks.

Cinderella's pretty little shoe, the good doctor goes on in some frustration, "is a most complex symbol....Since for over two thousand years...all over the world in much loved stories the female slipper has been accepted as a fairy tale solution to the problem of finding the right bride, there must be a good reason for it. The difficulty in analyzing the unconscious meaning...."

Pietro Yantorny, Shoe, circa 1912, Paris, France. Silk velvet (Italian or Spanish, 17th century), metallic buckle, glass beads, leather. Courtesy of The Brooklyn Museum, 53.267.13a. Gift of Mercedes de Acosta in memory of her sister Rita de Acosta Lydig.

MODEL

(FEET)

TWO INDUSTRY GIANTS DIVULGE TRADE SECRETS

ABBOTT MILLER: So, what's exceptional about your feet?
MICHAEL ALAN ROSS: I think the shape of the nail, and the shape of the toes. Everybody is interested in that and how it's going to look in a sandal. A lot of foot people can do shoes and socks if they have sample size feet, but can they take their sock off and still look good?

AM: That's how you separate the men from the boys?
MR: Exactly. The bottom of the feet matter too, but a lot of it is in the toe nails.

AM: Do you have a maintenance regime for your toe nails?
MR: I have a regular place for pedicures. I do stuff myself, but I can never seem to do it as well as they do. I go about once a week, but I'll skip a week if I am not shooting.

AM: Do you put a protective coating on your toenails?
MR: No, I stay away from that because it causes so much reflection. Working on your feet is just like working on a car. You get a little rough spot and you sand it down, and you put a little moisture on it, then you buff it and polish it. It's exactly like working on cars, the same principles. For example, buffing rouge. Well, what is it? It's just like if you are taking the scratches out of a car. And the little buffing cloth, what is it? It's a little piece of chamois.

AM: For your little Cadillacs?
MR: Actually I think of my toes as my little Porsches.

AM: What kind of shoes do you prefer?
MR: An old pair of suede cowboy boots; they feel like an old '57 Chevy. It's like slipping into a very comfortable garage.

AM: How active is your foot modeling career?
MR: I am always doing something with feet. I'm always doing a few shoots a week—it might be shoes or socks. The bare foot is less common than anything else. Out of all the parts I shoot, I think feet are probably the hardest. And socks are *really* difficult.

AM: Why is that?
MR: You have to make the sock look good. You have to make the foot look natural. And a lot of times in order to do that, it will look like you are standing up, but you actually have all your weight off of your feet. So you have to have a strong upper body to support yourself. Often I am flat on my back, or my feet are straight up in the air. So when your feet are up and suspended, and it takes all the pressure, all the veins out of your feet. Whether you are shooting hands or you are shooting feet, you are fighting gravity with your veins. If you are standing up, all the blood is going to rush down and the vascularity is just going to go crazy. Your foot starts to look really ugly.

MICHAEL ALAN ROSS:

"I remember flying into LAX and getting off the plane and seeing this huge billboard of my feet."

AM: So veins are considered unpleasant?

MR: It's funny, it depends. If you look at Michelangelo's *David*, he has one hand up, which is very graceful and the blood is all flowed out of the hand. The other hand is down and full of veins, and looks very strong. So if you are trying to get a beauty shot of the foot, it's better to elevate the foot and shoot it upside down and have all the pressure and the blood out of it. I'm giving you all my trade secrets here. If you are looking for strength, like a dancer's foot, then you are going to want the pressure on there, because it shows the power and the strength through the weight and vascularity.

AM: Are there any big campaigns that you've done, where we might recognize your feet?

MR: Remember those Fosters Lager ads that had a foot in a sandal on a beach? There were huge billboards everywhere. That was my foot and the ads said, "Australian for galoshes," or something like that. I remember flying into LAX, and getting off the plane and coming out and there's this huge billboard of my feet.

AM: What about film or T.V., or being a body double?

MR: I've done body double stuff with Charlie Sheen. We're very similar.

AM: Are your parts insured?

MR: Sure, but I won't disclose the amount because they base that on your income.

AM: Do you wear any protective footwear?

MR: Instead of waking up and stumbling across the floor and stubbing my toe, I tend to put my shoes on right away. I have to think about it all the time. I wear protective socks, and I buy shoes that are a little bit larger and roomier, because I use a sock with a double cushion in it. If I'm going out at night, or if it's a dress shoe, I'll wear a sports sock but I'll put a dark sock over it, so you don't see that it's under there.

AM: Do you believe in reflexology?

MR: I believe in reflexology. I love being touched. I did a book for a reflexologist, and at one point, I was just amazed. She pressed my foot in a certain place and I looked at her and I asked, "Should I feel like I am floating six inches off this table?" I wasn't levitated, but I actually felt like my body lifted up. It was just such a wild thing.

AM: What is the most fun you've had on a job?

MR: Don't go there.

AM: Have you ever been photographed for fetishist publications?

MR: No, I haven't. This is probably the weirdest thing, draping grapes on my feet. I think this is the ultimate.

ELLEN SIROT:

"People sometimes become obsessed with my feet, really pawing them and saying they're beautiful."

ABBOTT MILLER: How long have you been a foot model?

ELLEN SIROT: I've been doing this for seven years now. I started doing head shots and trying to get more commercial work. A photographer told me I have beautiful legs and that I should find out about parts modeling. I went to an agent who looked me over and said my legs were great, but my feet are perfect.

Of course, I never really suspected that. So the first thing she sent me out on was for Dr. Scholl's. I thought well, I'm never going to get this, but I went, and they looked at fifty pairs of feet and they chose mine!

So once I knew that I had good feet, then I really started taking care of them. I have a regimen that I follow every day. I apply cream, massage them a certain way, and do little exercises. But the really important thing is the choice of shoes. I never wear high heels, I usually always wear sneakers or flat shoes that are about one size too big. I always wear cotton socks.

Once in awhile, I have to go to something where I have to wear high shoes, so I will have someone drive me to the door. Then, I take my shoes off during dinner and have bare feet under the table. Then as I'm walking out, I take off the shoes or, I make my husband carry me or give me a piggy back ride.

I really work my feet into my lifestyle. I don't even think about it, I just do it. This is a twenty-four-hour-a-day job, it's not just when I'm on the set. I'm taking care of my feet every single minute of the day, because if I get one little callus, or a splinter or a cut, I'm going to be out of work for a month.

AM: You mentioned an exercise regime?

ES: Mostly, it's kind of a beauty care. I massage them with a mixture of sugar and olive oil to exfoliate the skin. I rub that on every night. Then I push the cuticles, and I put on moisturizer many times through the day.

AM: Many times through the day?

ES: Oh yes, probably ten times a day. I sleep with my feet elevated.

AM: How do you do that?

ES: I just put some pillows underneath. Because you try to have your feet above your heart as much as possible, it keeps the veins down and the blood out of them. I don't run or do anything aerobic.

AM: Have you been photographed for fetish publications?

ES: No, but a lot of people who you wouldn't expect when I'm on modeling jobs will all of a sudden become very obsessed with my feet. Just really pawing them. And saying, "Oh, they're so beautiful," and touching them.

AM: Do you experience a kind of detachment of your feet from yourself?

ES: On jobs I do. When I end up on a set, and they're talking to the foot: "Move the foot, tell the foot to move here. Move that toe." It's as if they have their own personality. They become their own entity, definitely. Also, when I go on auditions, you become protective, and take it very personally, when someone doesn't like your feet, or you don't get the job. Sometimes it gets way over the top, and you think, "Oh my gosh, my feelings are so hurt, my feet didn't get this job." You have to kind of have a reality check on it.

AM: So it's pretty competitive?
ES: Yes, like any part of the modeling industry. There are just a few people who are really doing it, so you really know who you're up against most of the time. And some of the jobs are very high paying. So, it becomes quite competitive.

AM: So are the top foot models ten people, twenty people?
ES: Probably about ten people. Not even ten people. There are ten people who are really doing a lot of hands. There are probably four or five people who are doing feet.

AM: Do you have a preferred shoe manufacturer or shoe designer?
ES: Keds or Dr. Scholl's.

AM: When you have to wear high heels, do you enjoy that?
ES: No, it's a scary experience. I get so freaked out about having to wear high heels that I don't enjoy it. I got married in little white sneakers, lace sneakers.

AM: Lace sneakers?
ES: Yes, little white eyelet sneakers with lace bows.

Ellen Sirot's foot. Photographed by James Wojcik.

AM: In writing *Footsucker*, what was the extent of your research into the subject of fetishism?

GN: I'm the kind of person who does research anyway, in my life as well as my writing. I get stuck on something, and I run with it as far as I can go. My preference is always to have a nonfiction element in my books, for two reasons: It's always interesting, and even if someone hates my book, they take something away from it. But also I like to blur fact and fiction. I wrote a book called *Still Life with Volkswagens* on the history of the Volkswagen, and some of the things are made up, and others are based on fact. For instance, Adolf Hitler used to collect model Volkswagens. And the factual elements obviously give it an extra authenticity.

Footsucker is slightly different because it's written in the first person, and the character I am creating is obsessive, but he is a student of his own obsession. There is a lot of comedy in it, and one of the things that drives the comedy is the fact that he is very rational, and he is trying rationally to explain away this completely irrational obsession. That's the kind of character that I wanted to write about. This is more interesting to me than someone totally inside of their obsession, with no perspective. I went to a fetish club in the interest of research, and there was this unattractive middle-aged guy standing outside the ladies' toilet, and he had a shoe in his hand, and as women went into the lavatory he would offer them the shoe and say, "Would you fill this up for me?" Obviously this guy has a story, but it wasn't the story I wanted to tell. He wasn't a student of his own obsession—he just did it. What you do as a novelist, as an artist, is that you are both in it and outside of it.

AM: There are autobiographical aspects in your *Volkswagen* book, and with *Footsucker* I found myself implicitly making the assumption that you, Geoff Nicholson, are a fetishist.

GN: Obviously, you're not going to write a novel like this if you don't have an inkling of interest. I guess I'm—well, you know the difference between a partialist and fetishist? A true fetishist would be perfectly happy with a shoe just as much as a person. Neither I nor my hero [the protagonist] is exactly that. He, and indeed I, are quite happy to have sexual relations with women who are not wearing high heels, or whose feet are less than perfection. Having spent a year inside this guy's head, I became utterly convinced that I was not a fetishist. But yes, I guess I am a partialist. Why else would I be writing about it?

AM: Have you seen Valerie Steele's book *Fetish: Fashion, Sex, and Power*? She makes the point that the literature on fetishism has largely ignored the design and style of fetish fashion. As a fashion historian, her approach is different from a literary or psychoanalytic perspective.

GEOFF NICHOLSON, AUTHOR OF
FOOTSUCKER, TALKS FESTISHISM
WITH J. ABBOTT MILLER

GN: When I was writing the character of Harold, who makes these outrageous, sexual shoes, I realized the day was coming when I would have to sit down and mentally design the shoes. The one that everybody likes is the shoe that has a snake's open mouth as a peep toe.

Someone has optioned the movie rights, and if the movie gets made, it has got to look fantastic. We were talking about who we would get to design the shoes: Would you get a shoe designer, or would you get a visual artist and make something that doesn't have to function as a shoe, but exists as a beautiful object?

One of the things I found about the fetish scene in London is that there is a whole group of people who don't believe in it, they go to fetish clubs as a fashion statement. I look at magazines like *Skin Two* and *Ritual*, where there's a lot of very designed rubber and leather gear, and there comes a point where it's overdesigned. There is a Platonic ideal of what a shoe should be. And there is a certain convergence toward it as you try to make it more and more like that ideal. It seems to me that the true fetish object is not actually that susceptible to endless variations.

AM: **That there is a kind of type-form, and beyond that it becomes rhetorical?**
GN: Yes, rhetorical is a good term.

AM: **Apart from their elongated heels, fetish shoes of the 19th century are not all that bizarre, but contemporary versions are much more high style. There is a "fetishist style." Steele's book shows the seepage of that style into couture and street style.**
GN: There is no need to locate fetishism narrowly within a fetishistic setting: A woman walking down the street in pumps or ordinary shoes is able to press the same buttons—if it's the right shoe and the right foot. It doesn't need to be a kind of burlesque, a kind of drag. There is a certain kind of "fetish" shoe which everybody can recognize, but there is also the kind of shoe that would appeal to a fetishist that wouldn't need to be as extreme, wouldn't need to enter that realm where it has quotation marks around it.

AM: **So what do you think is the classic fetish shoe?**
GN: One of the things I discovered about fetishism is that "there are many mansions in my father's house." I look at some fetishist material and it seems to be about something different. I don't want to say anything libelous, but there's a magazine in England called *Footsie*. It has pages and pages of feet which I find absolutely revolting. The guy who runs the magazine seems to be into almost deliberately ugly feet. This seems a very long way from what we experience when we look at an art object, or from what my hero is interested in. On the other hand, the American fetish magazine *Leg Show* seems to be targeting exactly the right erotic.

AM: **Is the fetish shoe, by definition, high-heeled?**
GN: I would say so. But there is a guy in *Footsie* magazine who is into clogs. Please! The high heel changes the shape of the foot to make it— I mean there is something about this curve [Geoff is pointing to the dramatic arch of a 1950s Perugia high heel placed before him] that is very sexy, whether it's on a shoe or on a car or whatever.

Shoe fetishism is about displaying the foot, but it is also about enclosure. The shoe is one of the few garments that retains its shape when you take it off. Even when empty, it's still foot-shaped.

AM: That's what accounts for the pathos of a stray shoe on the side of the road.

GN: That *is* really disturbing, isn't it?

AM: The question of female fetishism is quite complicated: Did you come across any case histories of women as shoe fetishists who desire men's shoes or feet?

GN: There is a terrific book by Lorraine Gamman, called *Female Fetishism*, and she has done a lot of research. Historically, women are not fetishists. Obviously there is a kind of feminist theory that wants to have equal time. Gammon has come across very literal cases that display the same features of male fetishism. She is going for equal time. It puts a lot of theories about fetishism out the window. But women as subjects of male fetishists are everywhere. You don't have to go very far to find women who have had such experiences. I know a woman who was riding the bus in London and after she kicked off her shoes to relax, they were stolen. She debated whether to go to the police and finally did. They claimed a great deal of expertise about fetishists, and said her case was not unusual, since many fetishists like their shoes warm.

AM: What about the distinction between foot and shoe fetishism?

GN: For my hero and for me, there is a lot of overlap.

AM: At the beginning of *Footsucker*, you talk about an incredibly beautiful foot...

GN: Yes, I describe the character's version of it, although its not exactly mine. I was talking to a gay guy last night, who is a foot fetishist. And he was saying that he found his own feet very unattractive because they were like girls' feet, and the feet he craved had to be big, masculine feet. Strangely enough I—our hero and I—need feet to be a certain size in order to be sexual. A girlfriend of mine had very beautiful feet, but they were very small, and strangely unerotic.

AM: An American reviewer suggested you are more inside the mind of the fetishist than outside, and that such insidedness can be claustrophobic for readers.

GN: I resist that criticism. It's a book *about* fetishism, rather than a *product* of it. The "fetish community," if you can call it that, is very excited about it, which surprised me, because I would have thought they would want me to be *more* inside of it. They like the title as much as anything.

AM: What about its reception in England?

GN: Similar. There is a great deal of denial. Most reviewers begin by saying that they know nothing about the subject, but they'll review the book anyway. There is a lot of throat-clearing. Woman have an easier time with it, as I think they do in life. They say they know why I would write such a book, whereas men say they can't understand why I would write it.

AM: What is you next book?

GN: It's about *walking*. It's about someone who decides to walk down every street in London. In Manhattan, that wouldn't mean much because you just go up and down, but in London it would be quite a task.

footsucker

GEOFF NICHOLSON

*IN THE FOLLOWING EXCERPT THE HERO DESCRIBES A
FILM HE WOULD LIKE TO MAKE THAT IS PIECED
TOGETHER FROM VARIOUS FOOT-PARTS OF OTHER FILMS.*

It was always a work in progress, but here's one way it
might have run. Fade in on Mickey Rourke sprawled on a bed
stroking Kim Basinger's feet in *9 1/2 Weeks*, then cut to Dirk
Bogarde doing the same with Charlotte Rampling in *The Night
Porter*, but here they're on the floor and he's actually kissing
them, then to *Bull Durham* where Kevin Costner is painting
Susan Sarandon's toenails, cut to Goldie Hawn in *Overboard*
where her manservant is doing the same for her. Then the
shot from *Who's That Girl*, where Madonna's just been
transformed from the street urchin to the glamour puss and
we see her for the first time in a spangly ball gown, and the
camera starts at her feet then moves all the way up her body
to her face, but in my version we do a freeze frame on the
start of the shot, the first moment when Madonna's feet fill
the whole screen. Madonna, incidentally, has feet to die for.
Cut to the scene in *The War of the Roses* where Danny De Vito's
girlfriend starts to give him a foot job under the table.
Possibly then a collage of images from *Single White Female*
where we see the girls trying on and buying metal-heeled,
black suede court shoes, several shots of these shoes pacing
corridors, then finally (and not too credibly in my opinion)
the scene where Jennifer Jason Leigh kills Bridgit Fonda's
boyfriend by driving one of the heels into his eye. Changing
the pace, we have a brief shot of Katherine Helmond in *Brazil*
wearing a leopardskin shoe on her head, an idea borrowed
from Elsa Schiaparelli, then Alan Howard stroking Helen
Mirren's feet in *The Cook, The Thief, His Wife and Her Lover*.

I could go on and on, but for now I'd end with the shot
from Buñuel's *L'Age d'Or*, when Lya Lys, in a state of sexual
arousal and frustration, sucks the toe of a statue of Christ. Her
lips are a perfect shiny black against the white stone of the
statue, and her eyes look glazed and orgasmic. It is one
of the most truly pornographic images I know. The only
problem with this, of course, is that it's a man's toe she's
sucking and that is well outside my range of interests.

Geoff Nicholson, *Footsucker* (Woodstock, NY: Overlook Press, 1996).
Originally published in the United Kingdom by Victor Gollancz.

FOR HEAVEN'S SAKES, you say to yourself at this point, He doesn't get it! This was written by a man sitting at his desk wearing orthopedic clunkers, maybe even the kind that lace up the side. Dr. Bettelheim probably *knew* Dr. Scholl. He never felt a pair of shoes slip themselves onto his feet and heard them whisper, "I am yours, I am you." Well Bruno Bettelheim, meet Bruno Magli.

Then he asked me what you looked like, and when I mentioned your silver shoes he was very much interested. (Baum, p. 127)

Some say that women wear high-heeled shoes (you know the kinds—stilettos, ankle straps, strippy naked-looking sandals) to inspire lust. In some of our lives, at some point or other, this is true, although I rather think that it is the undergarments such shoes suggest that are the real draw in these situations, with the following two exceptions: shoe fetishists—the ones who want the containers, not the things contained and will steal off with your espadrilles in the night; and foot men, who are actually deeply interested in feet. (I know about this because I had a long and very happy relationship with a handsome male who adored shoes and feet. He was a cocker spaniel.) But whatever carnal desire footwear inspires in men is nothing compared to the lust inspired in women: Desire for shoes. Hunger for shoes. Passion for shoes. Need for shoes. Craving for shoes. Yearning for shoes. Shoe fantasies. Shoe stories. (Shoe stores!) Shoe memories. Shoe mourning.

Near the end of L. Frank Baum's book, after her magic shoes had swept our heroine away from Oz and back to Kansas, something interesting happened:

Dorothy stood up and found she was in her stocking feet. For the Silver Shoes had fallen off in her flight through the air, and were lost forever in the desert. (Baum, p. 259)

(I know just how she felt. I haven't been able to find my black leather mid-heel pumps for months.) Should you happen to find Dorothy's shoes some day, slip them on. If you find them to be just your size, that is part of their uncommon magic.

"I wonder if they will fit me," she said to Toto. "They would be just the thing to take a long walk in, for they could not wear out." She took off her old leather shoes and tried on the silver ones, which fitted her as well as if they had been made for her. (Baum, p. 32)

If you also find them to be marvelously becoming, that is only ordinary shoe magic, as old as Eve, without whom we would still be naked. When we lost Eden, we gained evening shoes.

NANCY DALVA contributes to *The New Yorker* and other publications.

Pietro Yantorny, Shoe, circa 1912, Paris, France. Silk faille, gros point needlelace (Italian 17th century), metallic buckle, glass beads, leather. Courtesy of The Brooklyn Museum, 53.267.14a. Gift of Mercedes de Acosta inmemory of her sister Rita de Acosta Lydig.

Martin Munkacsi for *Harper's Bazaar*, July 1935. © Joan Munkacsi. Courtesy of Aperture, Inc. and Howard Greenberg Gallery, NYC.

FOOTS

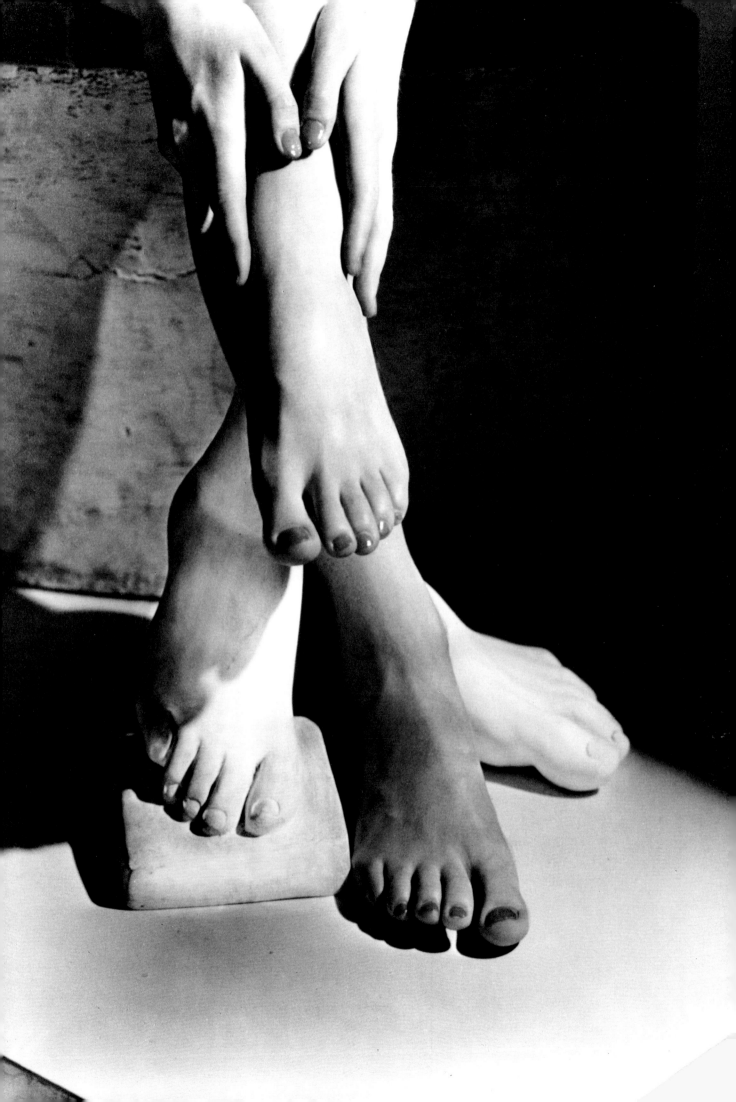

Horst, *Round the Clock*, 1987. Courtesy of the Staley Wise Gallery, New York.

Performance artist John Kelly as Barbette, the Parisian aerialist.
Photograph by Timothy Greenfield-Sanders.

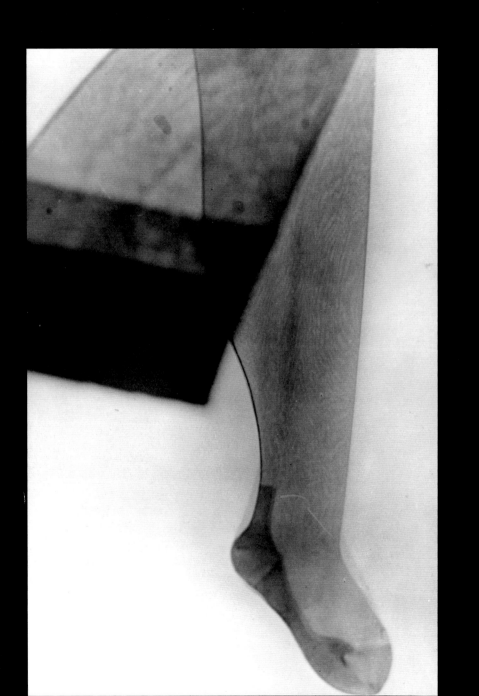

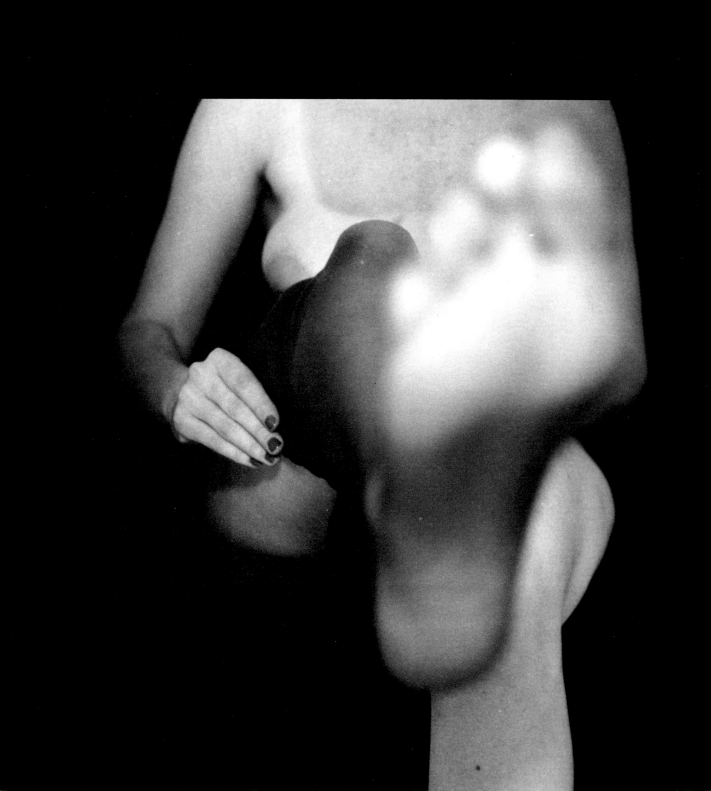

Max Yavno, *The Leg*, Los Angeles, CA, 1949. Courtesy of the Jan Kesner Gallery, Los Angeles.

Reshapings

HOWARD LEVY

The shape of your womb
is how I learned to tilt my head
when listening hard, when taking in.
Your legs, one slightly shorter
than the other (not enough to limp
but enough to sculpt the muscles
of your back and tense your walk),
took me through my first merengue,
taught those small refinements
of sway and balance
and life spread over me
simply, cell by new cell,
as light spreads over a shadow,
lessons of pace,
lessons of patience.

A dream that you are talking.
You hold a peach and tell me
about the luxuries of shopgirls.
1943. Lord & Taylor, the lingerie
and nylon counter. Twenty,
no soldier to worry over yet plenty
to meet, the jewelry of the jitterbug
and free to stay in the city overnight.
You phrase it, the shiny black satin
of becoming a woman.

How quiet we are, the two of us.
Each reading in our favorite
chairs, the rainy afternoon
moving towards dusk and
the making of dinner.
I am proud to chop the onions
and peel the eggs. I will earn
a small piece of cake, though

not enough to ruin my appetite.
How the afternoon we made
enclosed us.

And yet such loneliness chipped at you,
such a bleakness, as if everything
were too narrow,
people, ease, and the coronation
of desire, so that each day the loneliness
broke off some small edge of self
until the small, ruined abbey
of your heart lost its body's faithful.

In the hospital,
your legs elephantine with water
growing larger into your death
and my father and I
growing smaller and smaller,
unable to talk directly and honestly to you,
as if you were not
a dying woman
we both loved.

This first deep cold day of winter,
the air with no sense of forgiveness.
I clear some last leaves from your grave.
In a few weeks, it will be seven years.
Your grandsons are growing well.

It is so cold, and here in this cemetery,
I decide to imagine that you bear me
once again towards the vastness of the future,
while I remember and bear you back
in this tiny present, this brief
regency of noise and light.

HOWARD LEVY lives and works in
New York City. His work has appeared
in *The Gettysburg Review, The Paris Review,
Poetry,* and *Threepenny Review.*

Reshapings

HOWARD LEVY

The shape of your womb
is how I learned to tilt my head
when listening hard, when taking in.
Your legs, one slightly shorter
than the other (not enough to limp
but enough to sculpt the muscles
of your back and tense your walk),
took me through my first meringue,
taught those small refinements
of sway and balance
and life spread over me
simply, cell by new cell,
as light spreads over a shadow,
lessons of pace,
lessons of patience.

A dream that you are talking.
You hold a peach and tell me
about the luxuries of shopgirls.
1943, Lord & Taylor, the lingerie
and nylon counter. Twenty,
no soldier to worry over yet plenty
to meet, the jewelry of the jitterbug
and free to stay in the city overnight.
You phrase it, the shiny black satin
of becoming a woman.

How quiet we are, the two of us.
Each reading in our favorite
chairs, the rainy afternoon
moving towards dusk and
the making of dinner.
I am proud to chop the onions
and peel the eggs, I will earn
a small piece of cake, though

not enough to ruin my appetite.
How the afternoon we made
enclosed us.

And yet such loneliness chipped at you,
such a bleakness, as if everything
were too narrow,
people, ease, and the coronation
of desire, so that each day the loneliness
broke off some small edge of self
until the small, ruined abbey
of your heart lost its body's faithful.

In the hospital,
your legs elephantine with water
growing larger into your death
and my father and I
growing smaller and smaller,
unable to talk directly and honestly to you,
as if you were not
a dying woman
we both loved.

This first deep cold day of winter,
the air with no sense of forgiveness.
I clear some last leaves from your grave.
In a few weeks, it will be seven years.
Your grandsons are growing well.

It is so cold, and here in this cemetery,
I decide to imagine that you bear me
once again towards the vastness of the future,
while I remember and bear you back
in this tiny present, this brief
regency of noise and light.

HOWARD LEVY lives and works in
New York City. His work has appeared
in The Gettysburg Review, The Paris Review,
Poetry, and Threepenny Review.

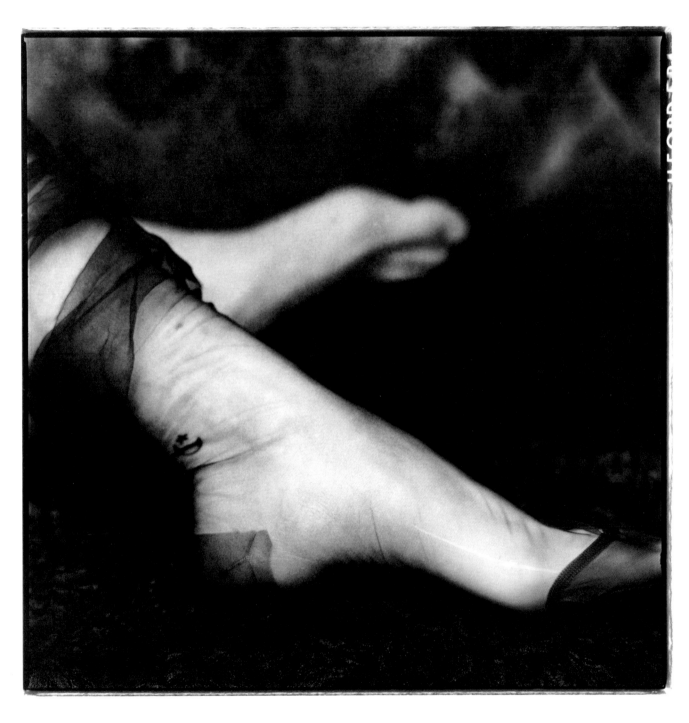

Keith Carter, *Moon and Stars,* 1989. © Keith Carter.
Photo courtesy of the artist and The Witkin Gallery, New York.

The relationship between the naked, vulnerable foot and its hard, shiny, artificial covering is both symbiotic and antithetical. But what if the differences between the foot and shoe should begin to melt away?

René Magritte's 1935 painting, *The Red Model*, depicts a pair of leather boots metamorphosing into a pair of leather feet. Used to illustrate the cover of the second edition of André Breton's book, *Le Surrealisme et la peinture*, Magritte's painting took on a three-dimensional reality in 1986, when Pierre Cardin created a pair of men's shoes based on the concept of the foot-shoe metamorphosis.

This image provides a clue to understanding both the visceral erotic power of shoes and the reason why shoes have been a favorite subject of Surrealist art. Although it is fashionable today to dismiss Freud, the unconscious significance of the body—and parts of the body—has long been recognized by artists and anthropologists, as well as psychiatrists. It is easy to laugh at cliches about high heels being phallic symbols. But there is ample evidence that the sexual symbolism of the foot and the shoe is psychic reality, albeit one that is far more complex than the usual Freudian scenario would have it.

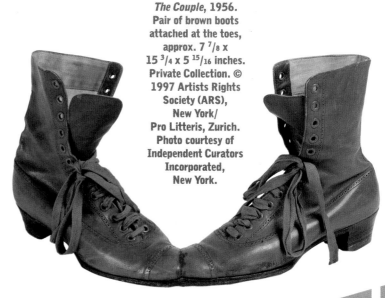

Meret Oppenheim
The Couple, 1956.
Pair of brown boots attached at the toes, approx. 7 7/8 x 15 3/4 x 5 15/16 inches. Private Collection. © 1997 Artists Rights Society (ARS), New York/ Pro Litteris, Zurich. Photo courtesy of Independent Curators Incorporated, New York.

fre
sli

Barefoot in the Grass Sandal by Beth Levine, circa 1968. Astroturf, clear vinyl. Manufactured by Herbert Levine, Inc. Courtesy of The Brooklyn Museum, 1994.40.5a. Gift of Beth Levine in memory of her husband Herbert.

Feet are always potentially, and often in fact, both a source of erotic pleasure to the person of whose body they are a part, and a source of erotic attraction to others. For example, one of the quintessential experiences associated with being "barefoot" is the sensation of grass against the soles of the feet. The sensitivity of the feet, the way they respond to tactile stimuli, is powerfully evoked in Beth Levine's "Barefoot in the Grass" shoes whose insoles are seeded with artificial grass. The tops of the shoes are clear plastic, reinforcing the appearance of going barefoot. The tactile pleasure experienced by the wearer of the shoes is derived by the stimulation of the nerves of the feet. But this is explicitly associated with the visual pleasure experienced by the viewer, who enjoys looking at (apparently) naked feet.

The libido for looking and touching is, in turn, accompanied by a process of sexual fantasizing. A case history in Havelock Ellis, for example, describes a foot-and-shoe fetishist who became excited by stepping on blades of grass, crushing them down, and then watching them rise again. The obvious Freudian interpretation emphasizes

VALERIE STEELE is chief curator of The Museum at The Fashion Institute of Technology. She holds a doctorate in cultural history from Yale University, and is the author of several books on the history and social significance of fashion, most recently *Fetish: Fashion, Sex and Power*, issued by Oxford University Press, 1995.

Toddler Shoe by Peter Fox, circa 199[?]. Leather. Designed in Cana[?] manufactured in Italy. Courtesy o[?] Brooklyn Museum, 1994.39.1a. [?] Linda and Pe[?]

dian
bers

surrealism in the service of footwear

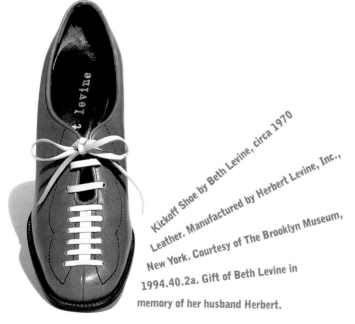

Kickoff Shoe by Beth Levine, circa 1970. Leather. Manufactured by Herbert Levine, Inc., New York. Courtesy of The Brooklyn Museum, 1994.40.2a. Gift of Beth Levine in memory of her husband Herbert.

the fetishist's castration anxiety: To put it bluntly, the grass can "get it up" again. But the erotic appeal of feet and shoes is overdetermined.

The Cinderella story provides the most famous example of how complex sexual symbolism can be. When Cinderella's stepsisters cut off their toes to fit into her shoes and are betrayed by a trail of blood, the subtext of castration anxiety is certainly apparent. But the story also emphasizes the idea of the foot slipping in and out of the shoe, an obvious metaphor for sexual intercourse. Fetishist pornography not only stresses the phallic significance of shoes (especially high heels and boots), but also the way the phallic foot enters the shoe, which, in turn, is often characterized by symbols of female attractiveness.

Peter Fox's "Toddler Shoe" provides a brilliant example of the symbolic power of shoes. One of the most popular icons of infancy are the small child's first pair of "real" shoes, which are sometimes even bronzed and lovingly preserved. By reproducing this toddler style in adult sizes, Peter Fox transgressively played with the ideas of infantilism and pedophilia, which have notoriously invaded other areas of fashion. Since the 1960s, the Lolita look of "baby doll" dresses, mini-skirts, and child-like accessories, such as stuffed animal knap-sacks, has become a conspicuous element in both high fashion and street style. Similarly, the impact of youth culture has contributed to the prevalence of extremely young and "waif-like" fashion models. The Toddler Shoes were controversial, precisely because they deliberately (and ironically) exaggerated our society's obsession with youth.

This, in turn, leads us back to the idea of the complex relationship between the naked foot and its artificial covering. Freud thought that the shoe was so frequently fetishized because it was the last (acceptable) thing the male saw when he looked up a woman's skirt, before his eyes met the horrifying sight of the female genitals. But in his Pulitzer Prize-winning book, *The Denial of Death*, Ernest Becker argued that "the foot is its own horror; what is more, it is accompanied by its own striking and transcending denial and contrast — the shoe." Whereas the foot is a low and dirty "testimonial to our degraded animality," the shoe—made of soft and shiny leather or colored silk, with an elegantly curved arch and pointed toe—" is the closest thing *to* the body and yet it is *not* the body."

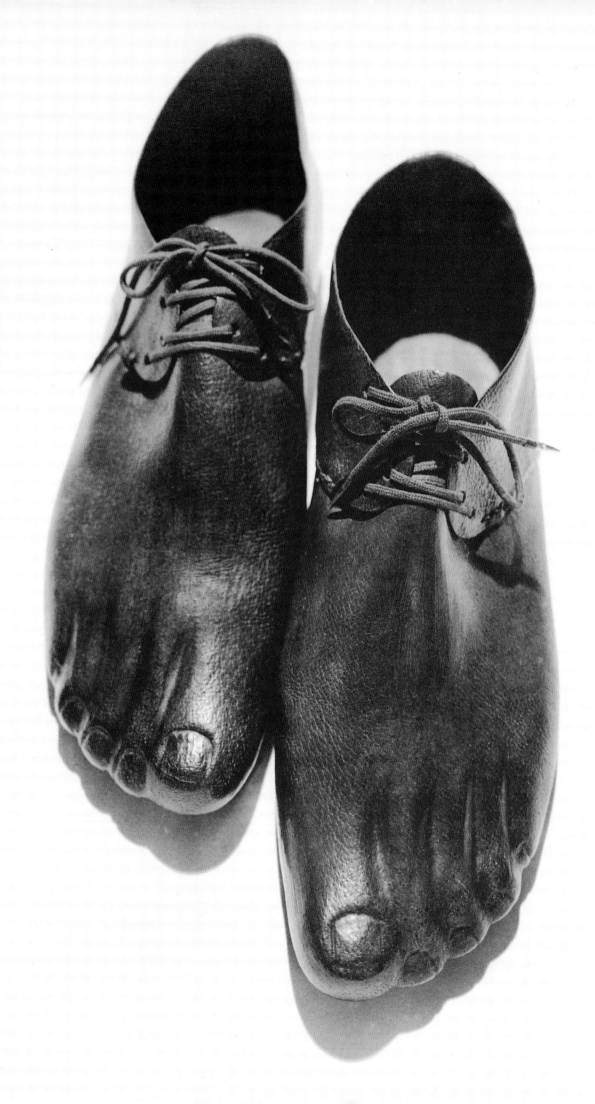

Pierre Cardin. Men's shoes, 1986.
Leather. Collection of The Museum at The Fashion Institute of Technology.
Gift of Richard Martin. Photographed by Jay Zukerkorn.

**SHOES MANUFACTURED BY
R. DELICATA, PARIS,**
designer and date unknown.
Courtesy of Robert Serling, New York.
Photographed by Jay Zukerkorn.

actual size

Mathias Fekete began working for the Sterling Last Corporation in Long Island City, New York, around 1951. His talent was carving lasts, the wooden forms on which shoes are made, which he learned in his native Hungary. During Fekete's tenure at the company, his wife fell seriously ill. While taking time from work, he began carving miniature shoes, mementos for his ailing wife. The sculptures, approximately 6 inches in length, were carved with an amazing attention to detail, their balance and proportions executed perfectly, as if they were models for real shoes. One Christmas, Fekete presented an example of his handiwork to his employer, David Serling. Serling was so impressed with this exquisite object that he asked Fekete for others. Over a 10-year period Fekete continued to create these remarkable shoes. His work is now part of an eclectic collection of shoe-related ephemera begun by David Serling and now maintained by his son Robert.

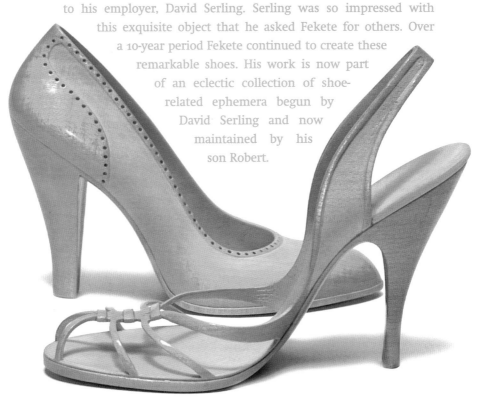

Mathias Fekete, miniature hand-carved wooden shoes, ca. 1965. Actual size. Courtesy of Robert Serling, New York. Photographed by John Halpern.

2wice welcomes the generous

Pages 9-12, 45-48, 57-60, 69-72, printed on Esse® by Gilbert, Gold, Smooth, 80lb. 118 g/m² Text; Pages 29-36, 81-82 printed on Gilclear® by Gilbert, White, 17lb. 64 g/m² Light

Cover: Mead Signature® Dull 100lb. Cover; Pages 1-8, 13-28, 37-44, 49-56, 61-68, 73-80, 83-92 printed on Mead Signature® Dull 100lb. Text.

support of **Gilbert** and Mead, leading manufacturers of uncoated and coated papers.

phone 212 228 0540

fax 212 228 0654

or mail this form to: 2wice 214 Sullivan Street 6c New York NY USA 10012

Name

Telephone

Address

City   State   Zip

Country

○ 1 year U.S. $36   ○ 2 years U.S. $72

○ 1 year Canada $46   ○ 2 years Canada $82

○ 1 year Foreign $56   ○ 2 years Foreign $92

gift subscription from :

○ Check [Make payable to 2wice magazine]